Stars of Pro Basketball

Here are the exciting stories of nine of the finest stars of professional basketball. Included are the triumphs and trials of Kareem Abdul-Jabbar, Billy Cunningham, Walt Frazier, John Havlicek, Connie Hawkins, Elvin Hayes, Spencer Haywood, Lou Hudson, and Jimmy Walker.

Stars of
Pro
Basketball

By Lou Sabin and Dave Sendler

Illustrated with photographs

RANDOM HOUSE • NEW YORK

To our wives and to our sons

This title was originally cataloged by the Library of Congress as follows:
Sabin, Louis.   Stars of pro basketball, by Lou Sabin and Dave Sendler. New York, Random House [1970] 144 p. illus., ports. 22 cm.
(Pro basketball library, 4)   Brief biographies of nine pro basketball players: Lew Alcindor, Billy Cunningham, Walt Frazier, John Havlicek, Connie Hawkins, Elvin Hayes, Spencer Haywood, Lou Hudson, Jimmy Walker.   1. Basketball—Biography—Juvenile literature. [1. Basketball—Biography] I. Sendler, Dave, joint author. II. Title.
GV884.A1S22   796.32'3'0922 [920]   73—117546
ISBN 0-394-80621-2   0-394-90621-7 (lib. bdg.)

CONTENTS

INTRODUCTION

....

Basketball has had to struggle to gain recognition as a professional sport. Through the years, however, it has had many great stars and personalities who have helped bring the sport to major-league prominence. These early stars often played under adverse circumstances and had far smaller incomes than the stars of other major sports.

But the times have changed. This book salutes the first generation of pro-basketball stars who will play out their careers as fully recognized professional athletes. Building on the contributions of earlier players, coaches, and owners, these young stars will continue to keep basketball in the forefront of professional athletics. The players in this book represent both the National Basketball Association and the younger American Basketball Association. Each of them has earned his place as a star in the exciting and demanding game that pro basketball has become.

Stars of Pro Basketball

KAREEM
ABDUL-JABBAR
by LOU SABIN

DECEMBER 1968 seemed a little early to start the 1969 war for college basketball's best talent. But not for Wes Pavalon, chairman of the board of the National Basketball Association's Milwaukee Bucks. Pavalon was determined to beat the American Basketball Association in the battle for 7-foot 2-inch Kareem Abdul-Jabbar, then known as Lew Alcindor, so he started bidding early and high.

"The ABA?" Pavalon scoffed. "Just how do they think they're going to outbid the whole state of Wisconsin for Alcindor? If all they can come up with is one million dollars, they'd better save it to buy themselves a one-eyed 5-foot 6-inch center out of Humpty Dump State."

Pavalon and the NBA got their man. The final price for the giant UCLA center was reported as $1,400,000. Once the 1969-70 professional season got underway, everyone agreed that Milwaukee and the NBA had landed a bargain in Kareem Abdul-Jabbar.

The Bucks were only in their second season in the NBA. In 1968-69, their first year, they finished at the bottom. But the next season, with their big rookie center they finished in second place only a few games behind the champion New York Knicks. Kareem had turned the club around and he was only a rookie.

Kareem Abdul-Jabbar learned he had to earn his

General Manager John Erickson holds up Kareem's first pro uniform. By signing, Kareem became a millionaire.

pay from the opening game on. As a newcomer with superstar stamped on him by the nation's sportswriters, he was tested—and tested hard—by the "big boys" of the pros. He came into the NBA thinking that he had control of his temper, that he could give and take the rough play of the league, and could just play basketball. As he discovered the night he came up against rugged Bob Rule of the Seattle Supersonics, he was wrong. In one of the first games of the season, Kareem erupted after a particularly rough exchange of elbows and shoulders under the boards. "John Tresvant hit me a couple of times," he recalled. "Bob Rule got a finger in my eye. Man, I just went for Rule. And I spit." Others had angered him, but it was Rule who infuriated him the most. "When I went for Rule there was murder in my heart," he said.

What did that teach Kareem, who was out to prove that his glittering past was only a prelude to a fantastic future? Was he going to play tough but unwisely? After all, he had once said, "It's going to be rough for me out there in the pros. But I might make it rough for them. It works both ways, you know!"

The answer came in a game played a short time later in New York's Madison Square Garden, before a packed house of 19,500. The New York Knickerbockers were driving downcourt, employing their fast break, when Walt Frazier whipped a pass to center Willis Reed, New York's pivot man. Reed snared the ball and muscled in for the shot, only to meet Abdul-Jabbar on the way. The two giants collided in mid-air, the ball flew wide of the rim, and Kareem came down reaching for the ball. Reed, however, wasn't interested in the rebound. It was Kareem he wanted. The 6-foot 10-inch, 230-pound Knick went after the young Buck, sending him stumbling backward with a powerful shove. Reed's fists balled as Kareem recovered his balance and started his counter-attack. Then, as if an inner voice screamed "Stop!", Kareem dropped his hands. The expression on his face made clear that the 22-year-old rookie had learned something since his run-in with Bob Rule. He was going to show he was the better man by playing a better game, not by answering violence with violence.

Reed seemed to see it, too, and there was no further trouble the rest of the night. Although Milwaukee lost the game, Abdul-Jabbar outscored and outrebounded one of the best centers in the pro league. Reed would later say, "How good can he be? In two or three years, maybe the greatest. He's got all the equipment. It's great to have the height and all those skills."

Kareem's 36 points to Reed's 11 echoed another personal court victory in his career, one that oc-

Kareem's ability to go up against the best centers, such as New York's Reed (white uniform), made him an instant pro star.

curred at the end of his second year of college varsity play with UCLA. The opposing center on that occasion was another strong pivot man, Elvin Hayes of Houston. The dramatic setting for their meeting was the semifinals of the 1968 NCAA playoffs.

Hayes and Abdul-Jabbar had met twice in their college careers. The first time UCLA beat Houston for the 1967 NCAA championship. The second time Hayes and Houston won 71-69, breaking UCLA's 47-game winning streak. But in this third meeting, for another national championship, Kareem completely overshadowed Hayes as UCLA won 101-69.

But his victories over Hayes and Willis Reed were only previews of what was to come. In the 1970-71 season, Kareem's second with Milwaukee, the Bucks were not content with second place—either in the regular season or in the playoffs. The team won 66 games, far more than any other team in the league. Then in the crucial playoff series, Abdul-Jabbar met Wilt Chamberlain, up to then the greatest center in basketball history. The young Bucks won four out of five games.

The next week, a few days after his 24th birthday, Kareem Abdul-Jabbar reached the top of his profession when the Bucks won the NBA championship in four straight games from Baltimore. Kareem had led the league in scoring through the regular season with an average of 31.7 points per game. And in the playoffs, his scoring, rebounding and defensive work made it easy for Milwaukee—they lost only two games and won twelve.

When he won the championship and established himself as basketball's top player, Kareem was still known as Lew Alcindor. But before the next season began, he announced that he had adopted the Islamic faith and an Islamic name. From that time forward he would be known as Kareem Abdul-Jabbar. Fans were sometimes puzzled by the change in names, but they soon realized that whether he was called Alcindor or Abdul-Jabbar, this young man was still *the* big man of the game.

Despite certain rumors, Kareem Abdul-Jabbar did not pick up a basketball the day after he was born, April 16, 1947, in New York City. And although he was 22½ inches long and 12 pounds, 11 ounces at birth, there was more reason then to expect that this baby would eventually go out for sports without too much body contact. His father's outdoor activities were swimming and track—sports requiring far more skill than muscle. But real height *was* in the family. Kareem's father was 6-feet 2½-inches and his grandfather was 6-feet 8-inches. In New York a tall youngster has to fight hard *not* to play basketball. Since Kareem grew to 6-feet 5-inches tall by the time he completed the seventh grade, a career in basketball was virtually inevitable. He had the muscle and skill to go with his height. At that point in his youth, he

jumped up and touched the rim of the basket during a game. After the game he stayed around till everybody left and tried it again. He did it thirty times in a row.

The rim continued getting closer. Along with his growth, Abdul-Jabbar's court techniques improved. Yet he still had things to learn about the game and the people who play it. Years after the event, he can clearly recall the day his Power Memorial team was going against Boys High, a Brooklyn school that perennially fields teams of considerable talent. "I was leaning over this cat," he said, "and all of a sudden I felt this pain in my arm. He had bitten me! The kid had just been beating his head against me for the whole afternoon, and he'd lost control of his emotions, and it seemed like biting me was just the thing to do. But what a bite he had! Nice and neat and even, right into the flesh of my arm."

So, along with everything else, Kareem had to develop a sense of humor or else the games would be twisted into one bitter battle after another. Without a cool attitude, he knew he could be driven to explode against a second-stringer and be kicked out of a game. In that case everybody suffered—Kareem, his team and his school. So he "cooled it."

In college the competition was tougher, stronger, more talented and more ambitious. But it was not

At New York's Power Memorial High, Kareem was the most sought-after player in the country.

too much for Kareem to handle. He was over the 7-foot mark and weighed over 200 pounds as a freshman at the University of California at Los Angeles. The spotlight was even brighter on the young star.

In his debut as a UCLA frosh, he demonstrated how good his college potential was. Opening at center against the UCLA varsity squad that had won the NCAA title the previous year, Kareem and his freshman teammates stopped them by the score of 75-60. His contributions were 31 points, 21 rebounds and seven blocked shots.

And his freshman season was just a warmup. In Kareem's opening game as a sophomore center for the varsity, the Bruins were facing a strong Southern Cal squad. UCLA had to play without two regular starters. Nevertheless, Kareem took charge, scoring 56 points and controlling play at both ends of the court. The USC coach had tried handcuffing him with a man-to-man defense, alternating a 7-footer and a 6-foot 6-inch player on the UCLA center. But all tactics had failed. Kareem kept on taking passes from his teammates and putting the ball through the hoop. In his post-game remarks, UCLA coach John Wooden said, "They'd be foolish not to give the ball to him. You go to your strength, and if he's not a strength, I've never seen a strength!"

Throughout his sophomore year Kareem dominated the national collegiate basketball scene. In a game with Washington State, he faced a center who

Kareem takes the net as a token of UCLA's victory in the 1969 NCAA tournament.

had orders to play him man-to-man. Kareem poured in 61 points. After the game, the center went up to his coach and said sarcastically, "Great idea you had there. I may go into the record books as the guy who let Alcindor get sixty-one, but you'll be known as the coach who was dumb enough to play him man-to-man."

Kareem's strength, skill and solid play increased over his three record-smashing years as UCLA's pivot man. By the time he was due to return basketball to the rest of America's college teams, he had scored 2,325 points, pulled down 1,367 rebounds, and was named Player of the Year twice.

Curiously, his debut as a professional was less than overwhelming. His behavior before each contest was strange to witness and he certainly didn't win the affection of fans. Like a nervous giraffe pacing inside a narrow enclosure, he would walk back and forth along the midcourt stripe, looking at no one, speaking to no one.

He showed signs of this behavior the night of his first professional game, against the Cincinnati Royals. Not only didn't he seem interested in the fans or other players, he barely touched the ball in the pre-game warmup period. Then, when the game started, the same distant attitude continued. Kareem won the tap but the Royals got the ball. Immediately, Cincinnati's Oscar Robertson whipped toward the basket, stopped and pumped in a one-hander. Kareem was nowhere near the board for a possible rebound. The Bucks took over and drove downcourt, with Kareem trailing the play far behind. Back and forth the players went, with the Royals building a larger and larger lead. Through it all Kareem acted puzzled, unsure, making only an occasional contribution to the Milwaukee effort. By the end of the first quarter Cincinnati had a 33-20 lead, and when Kareem's play didn't change in the second quarter, Milwaukee Coach Larry Costello benched him. The final score showed the Royals on top, 129-104. But when reporters tried to get answers from Kareem about his performance, he cut them cold.

He continued to be silent off the court, cherishing his privacy. But his feats on the court were public. By the end of that first season, he was second in the league in scoring and was third in rebounds, a sure choice as Rookie of the Year.

Then came the championship season. At one point the Bucks won 20 games in a row (then an NBA record). Then they breezed through the playoffs, beating Philadelphia, Los Angeles and Baltimore in short order. One of the reasons for the Bucks' success was the great Oscar Robertson, who came to Milwaukee in a trade before the 1970-71 season. His experience and play-making ability, along with Kareem's talents at center, made the '70-71 Bucks a classic team.

Some fans expected that the Bucks would continue to win championships for years to come. But in 1971-72 they lost in the playoffs to a great Los Angeles team. Kareem and Chamberlain battled throughout the series, but the Lakers, who went on to win the championship, prevailed in six games. Still, Abdul-

Jabbar averaged almost 35 points a game in the regular season to lead for the second straight year.

In 1972-73 the Bucks were upset again in the playoffs, this time by the Golden State Warriors, yet Kareem was still recognized as the top center in the league.

Bob Cousy, the ex-Celtic great and NBA coach, once said of Kareem, "He is the only man I've seen with the possibility of combining Bill Russell's mental concentration with Wilt Chamberlain's physical dominance." In other words, Kareem at his best may become the ultimate basketball player.

As for Kareem the person, his Buck teammate Guy Rodgers summed it up after getting to know Lew off and on the court. "This is a special kind of kid. I played with Wilt Chamberlain in the beginning and I've been in this league for a long time. Believe me, this kid is a rare human being."

Calm and confident, Kareem gets off his jump shot against 6-foot 10-inch Nate Thurmond of San Francisco.

BILLY
CUNNINGHAM

by LOU SABIN

BEFORE Billy Cunningham left for his first professional basketball training camp in 1965, an old
family friend, Frank McGuire, pulled him aside to
offer some advice. McGuire had made a name in the
coaching field both in college and with the pros. He
knew how simple it was for an outstanding colle-
gian, even one like Billy who had built up an All-
American reputation at the University of North
Carolina, to fail.

"I know what it will take for you to make it,"
McGuire told Billy, who would be trying out for the
Philadelphia 76ers. "The one thing the pros will
never forgive you for is not hustling. The day you
show signs of not trying, you just pack your bags and
go home."

Billy Cunningham went to camp with no intentions of going home. He was a scrapper from way

19

back. But he was also young, nervous and afraid. "For the first few days," he said, "I was sure I was going to get cut from the squad."

In the pre-season training sessions and in the first few games of the 1965-66 schedule, Billy seemed to be doing more things wrong than right. At North Carolina he had been a forward. But his 76er coach, Dolph Schayes, figured his best position would be at guard, especially since that was where Philadelphia needed help the most.

On defense, Billy was faked out of position and all too often opponents drove by him for layup shots. Or they got rid of him on "picks," cutting him off from the play and thus leaving the man he was guarding free for an easy jumper. On offense, Billy couldn't seem to handle the ball. His dribbling and passing were poor by professional standards; he often broke the rhythm of the 76ers' attack. He was hustling, but that wasn't enough. His worst fears were coming true.

But Dolph Schayes knew better, and kept Cunningham on the club. "After a few games," the coach said, "I realized that Bill would never be able to take full advantage of his potential—his driving and leaping—unless we moved him inside."

Billy's trial spin as a backcourt man was over. He

Billy, evading Willis Reed of the Knicks, was a frustrated player until he was moved to forward.

was shifted to frontcourt, where he bloomed like a flower taken out of the shade and put in sunshine. In eighty games of his rookie year, he pumped in baskets for a 14.3 points-a-game average. It was a high average on a team that boasted such scorers as Wilt Chamberlain, Hal Greer and Chet Walker.

"I got a big lift when I moved back to forward after Dolph dropped the backcourt experiment," Billy said. "I felt more at ease and began to feel more like a part of the team. I knew I could help more up front, not only shooting but also going to the boards."

Schayes agreed that 599 rebounds was a remarkable contribution from a 6-foot 5-inch tall rookie. In fact, Dolph was deeply impressed by Billy's all-around game. "He made picks, moved without the ball," the 76er coach said when he reviewed Billy's play at season's end. "He did all the things I like to see in a ballplayer. If he was played tough, he'd free himself instead of letting up. Billy's a schoolyard player. He's loose. He can give-and-go as long as you ask him. He does everything a rookie must do to make it big.

"First, he thinks under pressure. Second, he's a great competi or who loves to battle for the rebounds. Finally, he goes all-out, with or without pain, as evidenced by his play late in the season even though he was bothered by a bad back for almost a month."

Schayes, a native New Yorker, knew that Billy's desire to compete was standard basketball procedure for the boys who grew up playing in what has been called the "backboard jungle." Before he left Brooklyn to go to college, Billy wore out many a pair of sneakers in the warfare on asphalt playgrounds.

"Much of my jumping ability came from those rough-and-tumble beginnings," Billy said. "Basketball in the playgrounds is war and the New York guys have a style of their own. They're tremendous ball handlers and they are guys hard enough to jump out of buildings. In Philadelphia I've found that the kids can shoot better. But the New York guys drive a lot more. They go to the basket more and jump more, because they have to fight for the ball. So we learned to drive a lot, and fight for possession."

While Brooklyn's Flatbush section in the 1950s had its fair share of punks and street-fighters, Billy was not a roughneck away from the courts. He came from a family that believed sports was a healthy way of letting off steam. As one of four children of John and Helen Cunningham, he was taught to be fair and to share. So his early years were bounded by sports, school and growing up to be a decent young man. "I was luckier than some of the kids I went to school with," Billy said. "My father had a good, steady management job with the New York City

Fire Department. So we didn't have any worries about money and security. We lived in a nice house on a street with nice houses. Why, we even had a tree."

He also had a neighbor who just happened to be Frank McGuire's sister. Frank was then coach at the University of North Carolina. McGuire became a family friend of the Cunninghams and naturally was a close follower of Billy's basketball exploits at Erasmus High School. There, Billy was adapting his playground tactics to the hardwood floors and glass backboards.

At the same period in his life, he began to sprout physically, reaching the 6-foot mark as a sophomore and growing four more inches as a junior. By his senior season, Billy had added another inch and was converted from forward to center. The conversion was a smart move by his Erasmus coach, Bernie Kirsner, because Billy boosted his average to 35 points a game and the team put together an undefeated season, capped by the city championship.

"High school coaches deserve all the credit in the world," Billy said long after he had made his entry into the NBA. "They're the ones who make you develop the right habits, and these stay with you forever."

Cunningham and Kirsner also formed a friendship that lasted well beyond Erasmus High School.

Each summer, at a summer basketball camp they established in the Pocono Mountains of Pennsylvania, the coach and his former player relive memories of the old days.

Friendship with Frank McGuire took Billy directly from Erasmus High to the campus of North Carolina. The Cunninghams were so impressed with McGuire that their young basketball star didn't even give a second thought to the many other colleges offering him scholarships. So it came as something of a shock when McGuire resigned as coach shortly after Billy enrolled at the Chapel Hill school. Nevertheless, Billy decided to stay on. By the time his four years as a Tar Heel ended, he had acquired a degree in history and a place on the dean's list (he had started out in college as a physical education major), All-America rating as a basketball player, and a fiancée, Sondra Childress, whom he married after graduation.

Once out of school, he faced the big hurdle of making the pros. Playing for the 76ers but plagued by uncertainties, he didn't know he had it made until mid-November of his first season. In a game against the Boston Celtics, Billy put on a display of driving, shooting and rebounding that had the crowd begging for more. Playing as if he were back in a Brooklyn schoolyard, he unleashed forty-one minutes of perpetual motion. By game's end, Boston had lost and Billy had connected on 10 of 18 shots, plus six from the foul line, for 26 points. In addition, he picked up 15 rebounds. The fans bellowed their appreciation and Schayes put the final stamp on Cunningham's status by saying, "That was a two hundred per cent effort—the finest game any rookie has played since I've been here."

Billy's fiery play made him a fixture on the 76ers —but not a starter. Like John Havlicek of the champion Boston Celtics, Billy's reliable hot hand had earned him the role of "sixth man." Even though Schayes boasted of him as the best sixth man in the game, Cunningham wasn't delighted with the assignment. "It's tough coming in cold," he explained, "especially in tight spots. And you feel you have to tear up the court to stay in. If you miss a couple you start thinking the next chance might be your last. You hurry your move. You worry."

So Billy worried. At the end of his fine rookie year, he conceded he was satisfied with the way he had played and improved, then added, "But I hope I don't stay a sixth man for long."

In 1966, Alex Hannum replaced Schayes as the Philadelphia coach, and led the 76ers to their best seasons. During the 1966-67 season, they won sixty-eight games and lost thirteen, took the Eastern Division title and defeated San Francisco for the

Billy's ability to soar over opponents earned him the nickname "Kangaroo Kid."

NBA championship. The next season, Hannum led them to a 62-20 record and the Eastern Division title again. But the Celtics won the post-season playoffs and overall championship. Other than playing on winning teams, nothing changed for Billy in those two years—except that his game got better and better and his personal statistics climbed steadily upward. During the 1966-67 season he played eighty-one games (most of them as a sixth man), scored at an 18.5-point clip, and pulled down 589 rebounds. The following year, he logged 74 games, upped his per-game scoring to 18.9, and grabbed 562 rebounds.

Then came 1968-69. Wilt Chamberlain was traded, Hannum was replaced by Jack Ramsay, forward Luke Jackson was injured. Billy bounced off the bench into the starting lineup. His statistics as a regular in all of Philadelphia's eighty-two games of that year reflect the difference in how he felt. His scoring average zoomed to 24.8 points and he nearly doubled his personal high in rebounds.

Cunningham's new coach, Jack Ramsay, made a major difference. Billy really enjoyed Ramsay's type of basketball—a moving game. And without Chamberlain the 76ers became a fluid, free-flowing club that could fly when the fast break was on. With the middle wide open—meaning no Chamberlain clogging it—Billy's speedy, weaving, aggressive dynamism was on display game in, game out. No one could hold him when he was "on," which was practically all the time.

"You really can't handle Billy at his best," said a teammate. "The funny thing is, I don't think he can make as many of his shots when nobody's on him. He needs contact. And when he gets it, it's like he's playing with the neighborhood kids again. His eyes light up. He really likes going down the middle of the lane or across it, sort of like the way Elgin Baylor used to play—hanging up there and making shots under his arm and every which way."

Billy even went straight-ahead against Bill Russell, whose fantastic defensive tactics changed the professional game. But the Boston Celtics' center didn't change the Cunningham game. Cunningham scored against Russell just as he had against others.

What accounts for Cunningham's scrappy approach to basketball? "When pressure situations come up, I've got to admit they offer a great challenge to me," he explained. "I have to work as hard as I possibly can to get as good a shot as I can. We usually try to work some kind of play, but if that breaks down you've got to go on instinct. Are you going to try to drive and perhaps get fouled, or stop short and take a jump shot? You have to react without thinking, because you usually have only three seconds or so to make your play. You have to kind of time it yourself in your head."

The 76ers without Chamberlain were a distinct

threat to lead the Eastern Division again in 1968-69. The fact that they didn't win was no fault of Cunningham's. He played his heart out. He was named to the starting lineup in the mid-season All-Star game for the first time. In fact, he got more votes than any other player on the squad. After the season ended he was also elected, for the first time, to the All-NBA team.

Billy had reached the pinnacle of success in the NBA. His future looked bright. But Cunningham had a surprise in store when he announced his plans for the 1969-70 season. He said it would be his last in the NBA, for he had signed a contract to play for the Carolina Cougars of the American Basketball Association. The Cougars had made a very attractive offer, which included a higher salary, stock in the club, an outside business proposition, and a chance to return to his wife's home state.

But while the NBA and ABA had become heated rivals, Cunningham made up his mind to give the Philadelphians a 100 per cent effort in his last season. Scoring, rebounding, or defending, Billy went all-out. If anyone wanted to accuse Billy of letting up, all they had to do was count his bruises. While getting those bruises through the 1969–70 season,

With Wilt Chamberlain gone, Billy had to shoot more often. His scoring average went up and he became an All-Star.

he also got 2,114 points, good enough for a 26.1 per-game mark and fourth place in the scoring race. His 1,101 rebounds, a 13.6 per-game average, earned him seventh spot in the rebound race. Both records are remarkable for a forward and make it easy to understand why Billy made the 1970 All-Star team's first five.

After the 1969-70 season, Billy decided not to join the Carolina team in the ABA. He stayed on with the 76ers through a mediocre season for the team. Then the courts ruled that Cunningham would *have* to go to Carolina for the 1972-73 season since he had signed a legally valid contract.

His first year in the young league was spectacular. He led the Cougars to first place in the Eastern Division, averaging 24.1 points per game. He was in the top ten in scoring, rebounding and assists, and led the league with 84 steals. He was named the ABA's Most Valuable Player, adding another honor to his already illustrious career.

Cunningham played hard and did everything well. His drive and desire are illustrated by one play Billy made against the New York Knicks' Dave DeBusschere while still in the NBA. He took a pass from a 76er teammate. Without altering speed, he dribbled to the base line, faked Dave DeBusschere left, then right. Then he sneaked across the key, faked again, spun around and blasted toward the hoop. It looked like a certain, all-out drive for the layup, and De-

Busschere tried to match him stride for stride. He did—until Cunningham stopped on a dime, leaped into the air, and banked it in.

After the smoke had cleared and the 76ers had defeated the Knicks 140-137 in double overtime, Billy's total for the night was 44 points—a career high. "He was out of his skull tonight," said Knicks' general manager Eddie Donovan. "He scored forty-four points and he made all but six of them when our guys played him as well as a man can be played. Dave was on him, tough as nails, and he still got his shots off and made 'em."

DeBusschere added, "The only way I could have stopped him tonight would've been with a gun. And even that's questionable. The way he was going, he probably would have dodged the bullets!"

There would be other good nights for Cunningham, and other honors. He had proven Frank McGuire to be correct—there is no substitute for hustle.

WALT
FRAZIER

by DAVE SENDLER

WALT FRAZIER, a $100,000 rookie for the New York Knickerbockers, slouched glumly in his seat on the team bus returning from Philadelphia. He felt like two cents. Here he was, a professional ballplayer, and the precious few times he got into a game he just wasn't contributing to the team. Not with his shooting, not with his passing, not with his defense.

"C'mon over here, Clyde," said a voice from up front. It was Coach Red Holzman, calling Walt by the nickname his teammates had given him in recognition of his fashionable "Bonnie and Clyde" pinstripes and wide-brimmed hats.

Walt slipped into the empty seat next to his coach. "Listen," said Holzman, "I know you're better than you're showing out there because I scouted you in college myself."

Quietly Holzman lauded his 6-foot, 4-inch rookie

guard, then got to the point. "You're slowing down the offense by dribbling so much side to side," said Holzman. "If you've got to do all that dribbling, at least head for the basket. Try to penetrate."

Thus, Walt began to head for the hoop, regardless of the obstacles. Not too long after, the Knicks played the Philadelphia 76ers again. Frazier's "obstacle" was gigantic Wilt Chamberlain. Whirling left and then right, Frazier got a step ahead of his man, accelerated up the lane, leaped high and curled the layup around Wilt. Two points! Later, he drove up the middle and again challenged Chamberlain. Again two points for Frazier! "Willis Reed told me later," said Frazier, "that he turned his head one time and closed his eyes. He didn't want to see what Chamberlain was going to do to me." But rookie Frazier penetrated anyway. He sensed Wilt was hanging back a bit, waiting for him to pass off to center Walt Bellamy. Frazier put in 23 points and kept the 76er defense off balance with his ability to hit the open man.

That was during the 1967-68 season. Since then Walt Frazier has established himself as a superior playmaker, scorer, and defensive force. But even by the end of his first full season he was electrifying fans around the league with his dazzling versatility. When the Knicks played their final game in the old Madison Square Garden, for example, they saw their swift rookie driving and jump-shooting for

23 points, feeding off for 15 baskets, and going to the hoop enough to pull down 15 rebounds.

In his second season with the Knicks, Walt took right over as quarterback of the New York attack. He placed third in the National Basketball Association in assists (7.9 a game) and second among all guards in shooting percentage (.505) and rebounds (6.2 per game). He averaged 17.5 points a game. The statistics were impressive even if they didn't account for what seemed to be Walt's greatest gift—skillful defense. Though there were no published statistics to measure Walt's work on defense, the league coaches gave proper testimony when they voted him the NBA's Defensive Player of the Year.

Walt's standout play coincided with the Knicks' streak to the finish line in the 1968-69 season. The Knicks picked up forward Dave DeBusschere halfway through the season, then put on a show of team basketball that propelled them to twenty-eight victories in their last thirty-two games. While Willis Reed and DeBusschere were the productive workhorses up front, Frazier was the man who could light the fire and turn games around in a flash. The way he reversed the tempo of a mid-February 1969 game against the San Francisco Warriors is a good example. The Knicks were trailing by four points late in the third quarter and appeared listless. Enter Frazier, blazing hot. In directing New York to a 15-0 spurt, he scored nine points, passed to forward Bill

Bradley for another basket, pulled down two rebounds, blocked a shot from behind by 6-foot,
9-inch Clyde Lee, and stole the ball twice. All this
took place within three minutes. When the totals
were in, the Knicks had won, 98-92, and Frazier had
scored 24 points, assisted on 13 other baskets, collected 14 rebounds, and made 8 steals. "He's the
only guy who can strip a car while it's moving," said
New York substitute Bill Hosket, shaking his head
in wonder.

Warrior Jeff Mullins, who had connected on only
9 of 22 shots against Frazier, summarized neatly the
desperation a rival can feel when going up against
Walt. "You can't steal the ball from him and you
can't block his shot," said Mullins. "He's tough on
one-on-one and great on defense."

Many times Walt's defensive play broke open
games for the Knicks. In a late-season game against
Boston, Walt shadowed his man, Sam Jones, up the
court. Suddenly, Sam cut from backcourt toward the
basket. Walt ignored him, sneaking up instead on
the man with the ball, "Satch" Sanders. Sanders dribbled once. As the ball bounded off the floor, Frazier reached around Sanders and batted it away. In
the next instant, Frazier scooped the ball up and
buzzed the other way for an uncontested layup.

Once he was ordered to go for the basket, Walt's
scoring average zoomed upward.

Another time, during a game against San Francisco, Walt's teammates gave a classic example of how to exploit his uncanny quickness on defense. The Warriors' Jim King was dribbling the ball up-court and New York forced him to the sideline, limiting his passing lanes. Meanwhile, Frazier sensed that King was looking for the high-scoring Jeff Mullins and calculated just how King would have to angle his pass. When the ball was thrown, Frazier was there in a flash and New York went thundering off in the other direction.

When the 1968-69 regular season was over, the streaking Knicks had climbed to third place—three games behind the first-place Baltimore Bullets and one behind the runner-up Philadelphia 76ers. What happened next between New York and Baltimore astonished the fans.

The first playoff game was in Baltimore and the Knicks jumped into the lead. But the Bullets rallied early in the third quarter, pulling to within six points, 56-50. At that juncture, Walt Frazier put in three baskets in a row. Just to drive home the point that he could outgun the Bullets, he whipped in three successive shots in the first thirty-five seconds of the fourth quarter to give New York a 90-72 bulge. Still, the Bullets pressed on and trailed only 101-94 with 5:45 remaining.

Baltimore's sharpshooting guard Earl "The Pearl" Monroe tried to take over and bring the Bullets back with some fancy dribbling and shooting. Frazier crowded him, dogging Monroe's every move and straining to deflect his dribble. Earl was unable to score again in the game. New York won, 113-101. Frazier had 26 points, 11 assists, and 7 rebounds.

The Knicks went on to astound the basketball world by sweeping four straight from Baltimore. A couple of Frazier's moves in the third game—in which he scored 26 and amassed 17 assists—demonstrated why people were starting to call him one of the NBA's premier athletes.

New York was down by four in the fourth quarter when Frazier drove on Monroe and went up for the shot. Earl fouled him, and, while still up in the air, Walt shifted the ball to his other hand—away from Monroe—and put the shot in the basket. Frazier added his foul shot for the three-point play.

Minutes later, Frazier drove up the middle and beat his man going to the basket. But as Walt went up for the lay-up, Bullet center Wes Unseld dropped off to get him. With Unseld on his right, Frazier switched the ball from his right hand to his left and angled the ball in off the boards.

The Knicks played gallantly against Boston in the Eastern Division finals. Down 3-1 in games, New York struck back with a 112-104 win and seemed to be building momentum. But Frazier, who had gotten 23 points, 12 rebounds, and 9 assists, pulled a groin muscle near the end of the game. The injury

Frazier takes a breather during a time-out.

undoubtedly affected the Knicks' elimination in the next game with Boston, for Walt couldn't play his kind of basketball. On defense, he couldn't fall back quickly enough. He couldn't position himself and react speedily enough to pilfer Celtic passes and dribbles. He had difficulty staying with Sam Jones and Em Bryant in man-to-man coverage. Offensively, Walt couldn't penetrate and create the kind of movement the Knicks needed to set up good shots. Boston reserve Jim "Bad News" Barnes kept yelling at Walt from the bench, "It's hurting, Frazier, isn't it? It's hurting."

"I saw him holding his groin," Sam Jones said. "When I saw that, I started making my moves." Frazier played on, even as the injury stiffened. In fact, at one point in the game, Walt tossed in seven straight field goals. But the Knicks fell short, 106-105, to the team that was to become the world champion again.

Frazier came back fully healed for the 1969-70 season and the team picked up where it had left off. In late November, the Knicks faced Cincinnati with a chance to set an NBA record for consecutive victories. New York was gunning for its eighteenth straight. The prospect, however, seemed slight when the Knicks fell behind by five with just sixteen seconds remaining. But Willis Reed hit two foul shots and Dave DeBusschere swiped an inbounds pass at midcourt and scored. The Knicks were one point behind.

Still, it was the Royals' ball with the time almost gone. Miraculously, Reed slapped the ball loose. Frazier pounced on it, then drove furiously for the New York basket. He couldn't get all the way in, but he pumped the ball up with two seconds left. It missed. But he was fouled. Coolly, Frazier dropped in his two foul shots to give the Knicks the game, 106-105, and the record.

Though the streak ended the next night against Detroit, New York kept right on playing first-rate basketball. Frazier persisted in beating people with his all-round play. Frazier has lots of ways to win. One night he hit for 43 points. He almost apologized for not passing off more. "I've never scored that many points—even in warmups," he said. "But to-night I was the open man."

Against Detroit early in the season, the Knicks seemed doomed to a one-point loss, 111-110, until Walt reached into his bag of tricks again. New York had the ball with one second left, but as the players huddled during a timeout, the situation appeared virtually hopeless. Nonetheless, Red Holzman wasn't quitting. "We're going to run the one-second play," he declared. "Let's review where you go on this play." Out came the Knicks, needing nothing short of perfection to save the night. Knick guard Dick Barnett set a pick on Bellamy, freeing Reed to swing toward the basket. As Willis went for the hoop, Frazier arched his inbounds pass from midcourt. Up went Reed as the ball came in right on target, right on time. In one motion, Reed caught Frazier's pass and jammed the ball into the basket. The buzzer sounded and New York had a 112-111 victory.

The Knicks finished the season in first place in the Eastern Division and beat Baltimore and Milwaukee in the first playoff rounds. That qualified them for the championship series against the great Los Angeles Lakers.

In the fifth game, with the teams tied at two games apiece, New York's center Willis Reed pulled a muscle in the first quarter and was out for the rest of the game. Who would guard Laker center Wilt Chamberlain? How could the Knicks win without him?

In a remarkable team effort, New York won that game without Reed. Frazier controlled the offense and harassed the Lakers on defense, stealing the ball, intercepting passes and keeping them off balance. After losing the sixth game, the Knicks roared back with one more great effort to win the seventh— and their first NBA championship.

Walt's versatility dates back to his boyhood days in Atlanta. A quiet boy who excelled in all sports, he played every spare minute he could get. Walt was kept busy at home, too, because he was the eldest of nine children. He became proficient at handling babies and changing diapers, though he said, "After the third baby, I gave up the changing."

By the time he was in high school, Walt was a superb basketball player. But he was also an outstanding quarterback who could throw the football 75 yards. Indiana and Kansas universities wanted him for football and/or basketball. But as Walt felt that the professional prospects for a black quarterback were not too bright, he decided on basketball and Southern Illinois.

Neither the facilities nor the prestige factor at Southern Illinois impressed Frazier. But coach Jack Hartman did. Walt soaked up a well-grounded education in basketball. Hartman taught his charges discipline and fundamentals. He drilled the team endlessly on defense, setting the boys in a crouch and moving them around to develop their agility and reflexes. "We did it so much," Frazier said of those drills, "you couldn't straighten up. But if you didn't play defense for Hartman, you didn't play."

Walt played. During his sophomore year, Southern Illinois ranked second in the nation among small college teams. Coach Hartman found that he had to remind Frazier to shoot. "I've just never liked to shoot," says Walt. But he opened up more with his shooting to satisfy his coach. What Hartman clamped down on was Frazier's behind-the-back dribbling and passing. The coach said it was showboating. Walt disagreed, feeling it was sometimes necessary to get the ball or himself to a desired spot.

However, Frazier learned there had to be more to his life than basketball. He was declared academically ineligible in his sophomore year. He had been spending more time watching television and playing pool than on his studies. He made up the credits, however, and was back the next season with renewed dedication to both basketball and academics. Playing both guard and forward, Walt led his team to a 20-2 record. The reward was a bid to play in New York's National Invitation Tournament against a field of major college teams. The boys from Southern Illinois rose to the occasion. They swept to victory in Madison Square Garden, and Frazier, with his exceptional play all over the court, was named the Most Valuable Player.

Eddie Donovan, the New York Knicks' general manager, had scouted the tournament. Much later, after his team had drafted Frazier, he compared his evaluation of Walt with those of the other star guards that year—Jimmy Walker of Providence and Earl Monroe of Winston-Salem. "While we liked Walker and Monroe as scorers," said Donovan, "we really were more impressed with Frazier's overall game. He handled the ball well, had a great sense of direction, and was way ahead of the other two on defense."

When the Knicks' chance to pick came up in the 1967 draft, they made Frazier their first choice and

paid $100,000 to sign him. He started well in the ex-hibition season, then injured his ankle and had trou-ble regaining his form. All this time, Dick McGuire was head coach and the rumors were flying that he would be replaced. The uncertainty of the situation didn't work to the rookie's advantage. It wasn't until Holzman took over and had the talk on the bus with Walt, that Frazier started to play up to expectations.

Now Walt is an All-Star, a player who will go out and get 20 points a game and eight or nine assists—not to mention the steals and rebounds.

Frazier's quick hands are a constant topic of jok-ing and conversation. Not too long ago, a friend of Walt's started egging him on, saying, "You know, Walt, my hands are pretty quick, too. I can catch a fly in midair."

"I can catch two flies at a time," said Walt.

"Pretty good," said his friend. "Well, Bob Cousy was so fast he could catch three of them at a time. What do you think of that?"

"That's good," said Walt. "My trouble is that the flies have heard about me. They won't come near me any more."

Maybe so. After all, there are plenty of big, strong men in the NBA who shy from Frazier. They've heard about him, too.

Frazier developed into one of the finest all-around players in the game. Here he gets a shot off against the Chicago Bulls and draws the foul, too.

JOHN HAVLICEK

by LOU SABIN

THE sixth game of the 1968-69 Eastern Division playoffs was down to its final minutes. The Boston Celtics were leading the New York Knickerbockers three games to two in the best-of-seven series. But if the Knicks took this one they would carry the Celts into a seventh game with a fine opportunity to dethrone the National Basketball Association champs. Now, late in the fourth quarter, the score read, Boston 101, New York 99. The Celtics' John Havlicek held the ball with two seconds left on the 24-second clock. Suddenly he went up and let fly. *Swish!* The Celtic lead was up to four points.

The Knicks came back with a fast two-pointer. Once more the pressure was on Boston. And once more, with five seconds left on the time-clock, Havlicek had the ball. The fans were frantic, screaming, "Shoot!" But the Boston star coolly glanced at the clock, wasted *another* three seconds dribbling, then swept to the baseline, jumped, and hit the bucket. That made it Boston 105, New York 101. The final score showed the Knicks only one point behind, 106-105, and if not for Havlicek's key, time-consuming baskets . . .

"Well, the first one was kind of a prayer shot," Boston's hero said after the game. "I just wanted to get it up near the rim. The clock was running out and I figured we'd get a chance for the rebound, even if the shot didn't go in." Reporters pressed him to stop being modest, to confess that he had been worried or tense in those make-or-break moments. Instead, Havlicek grinned and went on to describe the second shot. "Now, on that last one I could have taken the fifteen-footer, only when I looked at the clock I saw there were five seconds left. That's an awful long time in that situation. So I used up a little more time, then shot."

Less nonchalant about Havlicek's heroics was Bill Russell, Boston's playing coach. "That first one," Russell raved, "was a crazy, wild shot. An unbelievable shot. The second one was the masterful play of a seasoned professional who knew exactly what he had to do, how much time he had to do it—and did it."

John Havlicek's competitiveness dates back to the first day he entered sports. For no matter what game he played, his intention was always the same—win. "The day I play a game and it doesn't matter whether I win or lose," he said in his serious way, "that's the day I retire."

Born on April 8, 1940, in little Martin's Ferry, Ohio, John didn't let too much time pass before he began showing his athletic talents. He spent his boyhood years hunting and fishing, enjoying the outdoor life and building a body that worked like a perfect machine in all physical situations. As a teenager, he put the "machine" to the competitive test. Whatever competition he tried—basketball, football, baseball, track, tennis, swimming, fencing, golf—Havlicek seldom got beaten.

"John is the kind who would have made it big at almost every sport," Arnold "Red" Auerbach, the Celtics' general manager and former coach, has said. "You watch him swim—beautiful. And I would like to make a bet that he can throw a basketball harder and straighter than any man in the league. He would have made a great baseball shortstop. And he once told me he threw a football eighty yards—and he isn't the type to brag."

Bragging is just about the only thing Havlicek didn't learn as he grew up. At Bridgeport High School, the versatile young man starred at every infield position in baseball, and consistently batted between .400 and .500. On the gridiron, he played quarterback and earned all-state honors.

John turned down the opportunity to play football at Ohio State, a stepping stone to the pros. His favorite sports were baseball and basketball. In addition, he was a "B" student who felt it important to have enough study time to maintain his high grades. Yet, even though he passed up college football, John couldn't resist trying out as a split end with the Cleveland Browns of the National Football League after graduation from Ohio State. The trial proved unsuccessful and, typical of Havlicek's reaction to failure, it irked his pride to remember that single setback in his athletic career. Several years afterward, he said, "I didn't see anyone in the Brown camp who could catch a ball better than I could. I didn't have the college experience, but I could have learned. Coach Paul Brown put me in for only a few plays in one exhibition game against the Steelers. On the first play I was flanked to the right. It was an end sweep for Jim Brown. It was one of those picture things. I cut down the defensive halfback and Brown went forty-eight yards to the two-yard line." After the Browns scored, and the Steelers failed to gain a first down on the next series of plays, the Browns' offensive unit came in again. "The next time we had the ball," Havlicek continued, "I was a

Havlicek played a major role in making Ohio State one of the finest teams ever assembled. Here he hooks a shot against Kentucky.

John's tryout with the Cleveland Browns was short and uneventful. He was bitter over the treatment he received.

decoy on the flank. I ran my patterns but no one threw to me. And that was it. I didn't play anymore."

John revealed rare bitterness as he told the story. He is convinced that Paul Brown didn't give him a fair shot at the job. Red Auerbach agrees. "They had him at the wrong position," Auerbach said. "He would have been a great quarterback." It took Havlicek years before he finally got over Brown's "insult" to his talents.

Whatever the sport, fitness is a key word when the subject is 6-foot, 5-inch, 205-pound John Havlicek. He worked twelve months a year to stay in shape, to be more than ready for the next challenge. "I'm not the fastest guy in the game," he admitted, "so I have to stay sharp and ready to go every minute of every game. You'll see more players in our league standing at the foul line, and they're taking those deep breaths. They look like they're hoping they can make the free throw last two or three minutes. Heck, when you think you're tired, you are tired. I've never been tired in my life. Now, I don't really do anything special to get in shape, but I'm always involved in doing something. On the day of a game, I'll run errands to the dry-cleaners, things like that. In the off-season, I'm swimming, hunting, camping, playing golf or tennis. I never lie around and get the chance to be fat."

Thus, for Havlicek, there is no such thing as an "off-season." This approach to staying in top shape has dominated Havlicek's view of sports and, it seems, life in general. If there is a secret to John's success as an athlete, it is that sports are his work, his hobby and his greatest pleasure in life.

Commenting on Havlicek's almost superhuman stamina, author John Devaney wrote, "In game after game he physically beats some of the best-conditioned athletes in the world . . . the guards and forwards of the NBA. He beats them by running and running—and running some more—and they marvel at how he beats them, and they wish, Lord how they wish, they could run the way he runs."

Sturdy, tireless and ambitious, Havlicek arrived in professional basketball ready to do everything asked of him, and more. His scoring ability is matched by his pro-style defensive play, honed to near-perfection at Ohio State. But when he joined the Celtics for the 1962-63 season, he was so impressed by the sharpshooters on the team that he displayed an obvious reluctance to shoot. Finally Red Auerbach, the team's coach, advised him, "You're not helping us when you pass off and don't take your share of shots. The other teams know you're not going to shoot when you get the ball. Take your shot."

Havlicek started shooting, notching a first-year average of 14.3 points. But the combination of Auerbach's encouragement with his own enthusiasm also led him to go one step too far that first winter. "It was my rookie year, remember," Havlicek said, picturing the situation in his mind. "We were in the playoffs against Los Angeles, and I came into one game with that special enthusiasm of a first-year man going for his first title. Right off, we got our fast

John made the Celtics move the ball, but his shooting talents were what the team really needed.

break moving and I hit for six points. The team was rolling and then, scrambling to make a steal near the sideline, I tumbled into the stands and sprained my ankle. I had to miss a couple of games and I was really upset because I seemed to be going so well."

One year was enough to give Havlicek the feel of things in the big league. By the time he reached his eighth year as a Celtic, he was a member of pro basketball's select 10,000-points-scored circle. Yet his career average of close to 20 points a game merely begins to describe his value to the team. On a par with his scoring was his versatility. He became the best "sixth man" to ever play the game, for that was his role on the championship teams Boston fielded season after season. Once in the game, John would sink a series of clutch baskets, or stop the hot hand of an opponent who was giving Boston a hard time. He was a running machine, the man who kept his teammates from slowing up or growing lax on attack and defense.

"I've had to do a little bit of everything during my years with the Celtics," he said. "And I get a special kick out of helping out whenever I'm needed. I've had a lot of publicity as Boston's sixth man, but I also have been a starter. I've worked as a forward and as a guard, as a shooter and as a ballhandler. On defense, I think I've covered everyone in the league except the huge centers." To which Bill Russell added, just before he retired as player-coach,

"John's as good as any forward we have, and he's as good as any guard we have. And that's why he's sixth man. He swings, man. If one of the forwards isn't going good, you blow a whistle and in comes John. If it's one of the guards who isn't going good, you use the same whistle."

Havlicek summarized his sixth-man status this way: "Whether I start or come off the bench makes no difference to me. I don't change anything in the way I play. My game has always been to go as hard as I can as long as I can. I want my opponent to chase me. I want him to get tired and loaf maybe once or twice on defense. That's when I'll take advantage of him by getting the cheap basket."

"Cheap" baskets in Havlicek's terms would be well-earned ones in anyone else's vocabulary.

The retirements of Bill Russell and Sam Jones at the conclusion of the 1969 season changed Havlicek's role. Though they were the defending NBA champions, the Celtics were suddenly in need of a large dose of inspiration to make up for the loss of Jones and Russell. Without big Bill getting the rebounds in bunches at both ends of the court, it was up to Havlicek, as team captain, to go in and lead the battle under the boards. To no one's surprise, he did.

Of Sam Jones's sharpshooting ability, Havlicek said, "Nobody could get the basket better when a team needed it. We'd try to set Sam up in the last

couple of minutes if we needed a basket to stay in the game, or one to wrap it up." Nevertheless, Havlicek accepted this role, too. He finished the 1970 schedule with the highest scoring average of his career, 24.2 points a game.

Responding to pressure situations was always standard equipment in Havlicek's bag of abilities. Indeed, it was practically an insult for general manager Auerbach or anyone else to tell him what was expected of him. But John doesn't mind urging a teammate to play to his best ability. Just the year before, whenever Russell showed signs of slowing down in a game, Havlicek would needle the player-coach. "Russell would clear the defensive rebound," John recalled, "and then loaf up the court so that we'd have to play four-on-five until he got there. 'Russell, run!' I'd yell from the bench whenever he didn't hustle back on defense. 'You're no good to us if you don't come up the floor!' "

Not only did Russell run, the whole Celtic team picked up its tempo of play. Russell didn't complain about Havlicek's prodding. "I need that kind of push," Bill said. "Besides, I happen to like John very much. Even more than that, he's a great player. He gives you tremendous support."

Often the kind of support Havlicek gives won't

Snappy, hustling defense, such as this block against a Milwaukee Buck player, got Havlicek All-Star ranking.

show in the box scores or personal statistics. There a fan can read about points, rebounds and assists. Nowhere, however, do the record books show the kind of total support John himself described in a relaxed review of the high points of his pro experiences. "Nobody ever scored on the most dramatic play I ever made for the Boston Celtics," he said. "It came in a 1965 game, Boston Garden was packed, and the Eastern Division title was hanging in the balance.

"Many experts had said that Wilt Chamberlain and the oncharging Philadelphia 76ers were going to knock off the proud Celtics, and, sure enough, here they were with a pretty good chance to do so. Five seconds showed on the clock—five seconds and the playoffs would be all over. It was 3-3 in games, and, though we had a one-point lead, Hal Greer of the 76ers was about to throw the ball inbounds from under the Philadelphia basket. I figured they'd try to feed Chamberlain underneath. He would muscle his way to the hoop and either score or try to draw a foul.

"I was watching my man, Chet Walker, and suddenly I realized that Greer wasn't going to throw the ball in to Wilt. He was obviously looking for someone in backcourt. Instinctively, I crept a little closer to Walker just as Greer looped his pass toward Chet. I leaped high into the air in front of Walker and *thwack!* the ball slapped into my hands. It was our ball, our game, and our title. The buzzer sounded and from there we went on to win the NBA championship for the seventh straight year."

Another championship. Another trophy on the award-filled shelves in the home of John Havlicek. Another piece of evidence that, on the strength of competitiveness, John Havlicek ranks with the best to ever wear a uniform in the NBA.

CONNIE HAWKINS

by LOU SABIN

THE marquee outside Pavalon Arena in Milwaukee didn't even bother to mention that the Milwaukee Bucks were playing the Phoenix Suns. Instead, it read:

CONNIE HAWKINS VS. LEW ALCINDOR

Promotors had a dream match in the making between two of the most highly-touted newcomers in National Basketball Association history and they were playing it to the hilt. They knew that the fans cared more about how Hawkins of Phoenix would penetrate the defensive wall of Milwaukee's Alcindor (later known as Kareem Abdul-Jabbar) than what the final score of the game would be.

The 1969 exhibition game began with the Bucks' 7-foot 2-inch center keeping a wary eye on the smooth-moving Suns' forward. Hawkins, 6-feet 8-inches tall, 205 pounds, had been an All-Star center in the American Basketball Association, but he was giving away 6 inches and 40 pounds to the rookie from UCLA. For a while it looked as if there would be no moment of truth. Then something about the way Hawkins glided across the midcourt stripe stirred the fans. His slim, muscular body slid over the boards with the grace of an alley cat on the prowl.

Hawkins cut to the right corner, where a pass caught up with him. Connie cradled the ball in his huge right hand and burst into high gear, angling past Alcindor, who stood between him and the basket. Lew moved to intercept him but Hawkins twisted in midstride and went up for the shot. Even then, Alcindor recovered in time. Reaching up, up, up, Lew whacked the ball out of play. For a split second, disappointment registered on Hawkins' long face. Then his eyes glinted with satisfaction as the referee signaled goal-tending against Alcindor.

Hawkins went on to record 19 points, seven rebounds and five assists in the head-to-head encounter. In the forty-four minutes he played, he made 50 per cent of his shots, and connected on all three free throws.

The next day the sports pages declared that Connie Hawkins was everything everyone had expected him to be. "Another Elgin Baylor," reported one

Hawkins, shooting here against the Cincinnati Royals' Connie Dierking, was a polished pro star when he came into the NBA.

writer. "It's no different for 'Hawk' in the NBA than it was in the ABA," wrote another. A third review of Hawkins' debut stated, "The Suns will shine in '69. The 28-year-old rookie is a superstar."

How Connie Hawkins had become a superstar is a rags-to-riches story, basketball style. In 1969, when Hawkins signed a long-term, million-dollar contract to play in the NBA, everyone envied him the good life, the easy life. On basketball courts all over the country, young players were thinking, "That's what I want to be—another Connie Hawkins."

There was a time, however, not too long ago, when no one wanted to be another Connie Hawkins. "He's had it tough since the day he was born," confided a man who has carefully followed Connie's career. "If he couldn't play this game, he'd have nothing, he'd be nothing. Without basketball saving him, he might be a bum today."

Once one knows the Connie Hawkins story, one realizes just how lucky Connie is. In 1967, Hawkins had a wife, two children, and very little income. "I was worried," he said. "I was twenty-six and playing this game was all I could really do. Sure, I had a family to support, but my mind was infected with basketball. Always has been. I couldn't get too interested in doing anything else."

Poverty can do that. It gives a boy a low view of life, where school doesn't matter because education does not seem to pay off. Poverty makes life look like a long road of jobs with low pay and no future. Sports matter, though. Playing a rough-and-tumble game lets a boy blow off steam. It lets him forget there's not much food at home. It gives him hope— usually slim hope—that he'll be good enough to coach at some high school or college. Or maybe even be a professional athlete. And poverty was Hawkins' world, the only kind of life he knew in the Bedford-Stuyvesant Negro slums of Brooklyn.

"Of all the poor people I knew in New York," said Billy Cunningham, another Brooklyn-born star who made the big leagues, "Connie was the poorest."

Being poor was bad enough. But Connie also had other problems riding his shoulders when he was young. Born on July 17, 1940, he was one of six children who needed food and clothing—things that don't come often enough when the father of the family disappears and the mother is going blind. That was Connie's world when he was ten years old. Even so, he stayed out of trouble in the midst of junkies, gangsters, and the tremendous temptation to steal things in order to survive. He played basketball and went to school. Of course, school for him meant being promoted a grade every year without ever learning anything. Slum kids often move through the grades according to age, not marks. They can get a high school diploma and not even be able to read it.

Four years at Brooklyn's Boys High School furnished the tall, skinny boy little education. But school sports did give him a strong thirst for the fame and applause that the great ones get. New York City people are hot basketball fans, and 18,000 of them cheering, "Go, Hawk, go!" at Madison Square Garden can give a poor youngster rich dreams. Connie was flooded with cascades of cheers as he led Boys High to two straight city championships.

He also heard the cheers while playing for the East team in a 1960 All-Star game for high school seniors from all over America. In this contest, Hawkins' performance dimmed the lights of such future pros as Jeff Mullins, Joe Caldwell and Paul Silas.

Fog had made the outdoor court in Pittsburgh slippery. Puddles of water dotted the playing surface. The basketball often *squished* when it was dribbled and players skidded when they drove, twisting to the floor while the ball squirted in a different direction. One observer at the game reported: "Where others had merely walked on water, a graceful, long-armed 6-foot, 7-inch youngster began to run on water—then fly. And, all of a sudden, the game was no longer competition. He was grabbing the rebounds, as he had been doing all along. But now he was no longer pitching out to his guards to set the fast break in motion. Now he was scrubbing the boards clean and dribbling the length of the treacherous floor himself, leading the fast break and capping it off with dunk shots or Cousy-like behind-the-back passes to teammates as he floated toward the basket, drawing the defense with him.

"On a dry court, the sight of a big man rebounding, leading the fast break and capping it off with fancy assists would boggle the imagination, but on a wet court it defied belief. Yet time and again it was happening.

"The final score was East 85, West 60, and a tremendous individual victory for one young man. The man, the winner of the Most Valuable Player trophy in this game, was Connie Hawkins."

Despite his poor academic record, Hawkins received nearly 250 college scholarship offers. His dreams were on the edge of becoming reality. But a nightmare was developing.

Among Hawkins' rooters was a former standout basketball player named Jack Molinas, a lawyer. Molinas always seemed to be around when Connie played, whether it was in the high school league or on the playgrounds. Connie, along with a Boys High teammate, occasionally ended up as Molinas' guest for dinner. Molinas also lent Hawkins $200, which Connie quickly repaid.

The attention given by Molinas was forgotten as Connie packed his sneakers and headed for the University of Iowa, where he had a scholarship waiting. But the ghost of those free dinners began haunting

Hawkins when a basketball scandal broke in 1961 and Jack Molinas was named as one of the gamblers involved. Molinas was convicted and jailed. By the time the New York District Attorney's office had finished questioning the confused twenty-one-year-old Hawkins, Connie's name had become linked to gambling, too. His reputation was ruined. Innocent in the eyes of the law, he was nevertheless "guilty" because of his association with Molinas. At least, that was the way authorities felt at the University of Iowa. They cancelled Connie's scholarship. Also cancelled were his dreams of playing college ball anywhere else. No other school dared to contact him. But the most crushing blow of all was dealt by the National Basketball Association, which declared Connie ineligible, too. Until temporary salvation came with the formation of the American Basketball League, Hawkins was a man without a team.

Connie played for the ABL's Pittsburgh Rens and against some pretty strong competition, though just twenty years old, he ended his first season as the league's Most Valuable Player. In seventy-eight contests, Connie averaged 27.5 points a game. Success gave him security. He married and moved to Pittsburgh—only to have his world collapse again when the league folded halfway through its second season. The next four years were spent playing the endless day-and-night schedule of the Harlem Globetrotters. Apart from earning a mere $125 a week,

Connie learned three things in that time: (1) additional basketball savvy, (2) how to fool around with a ball and nine other clowns, and (3) what it could be like playing in the NBA.

"In my four years with the Globetrotters," he said, "Sweetwater Clifton, the ex-Knickerbocker, taught me a lot about ball-handling. I also went against a lot of NBA stars like Wilt Chamberlain and Oscar Robertson. But that was only now and then, on playgrounds and such. Anyway, I always felt I could hold my own with them."

To a man, the professional players agreed with him.

Connie's first real change of luck came when the American Basketball Association was formed in 1967. Connie was invited to play for the Pittsburgh franchise. The Pipers offered him a $15,000 contract and he grabbed it. In repayment, he averaged 26.8 points a game, led the team to the league championship, and was voted the ABA's Most Valuable Player. The next year, despite being sidelined by injuries and the flu, Connie earned All-ABA status by hitting for a 30.2 average.

But even bigger and better things were in store. Before the 1968-69 season, a Pittsburgh lawyer, David Litman, had instituted a six-million dollar suit against the NBA on Connie's behalf. The NBA responded by agreeing to give Hawkins a contract to play in its league—if he would drop the suit. In

making the offer, the league's board of governors said, "We simply had an indefensible stand. We had wronged this boy, if not by being party to the original act, by supporting it later . . . We wanted to right a wrong."

At last Hawkins was where he belonged—competing against the best players in the world. It was decided by the league that he would play for Phoenix. Now he could afford to live well, give his family some luxuries, pay for an operation that might restore his mother's sight. He could finally enjoy some of the dignity that had been denied him for so many years.

But there were more hurdles to clear. When the 1969-70 season opened, Hawkins was unsure of himself. He admitted to being somewhat of a worrier, but also insisted that his knee injury—sustained in his last ABA season—was still bothering him. "It's real," he said. "I don't imagine the pain." He was also breaking in with a new team and playing at forward, not the center position he had starred at for so long. But he was willing to change, to cooperate, to learn.

A teammate, NBA veteran Paul Silas, said, "Connie doesn't act like a star. He accepts suggestions. He gives them. He helps the young kids. He's going to

With the Minnesota Pipers, Connie was the ABA's best player. But he yearned for NBA competition.

have to learn to put out more, but he's going to help us. We're all going to be looking to him for leadership. I feel now that he'll give it."

Connie is a learner. His education began later in life than most people's, but he came a long way from Bedford-Stuyvesant and poverty. He learned to read and write, and to talk as an equal with men far better educated than he. He proved his desire and potential to learn back in his Globetrotter days, when basketball wasn't the only thing he studied.

"You couldn't pay enough to get all the experience I got with the Globetrotters," he said. "You played every day, and you learned ball control doing all those stunts. You learned how to travel and how not to get too tired to play. We went to Europe four times. I learned a little of the language of every country we played in. We traveled with a group of dancers in Czechoslovakia, and two of them taught me to speak Czech fluently. I can speak French, Spanish, German and Italian. I guess I have a good ear for language.

"I enjoy learning a new language. It used to bother me when people came up to us in Europe and I couldn't understand what they were saying. It felt good when I learned and could have conversations with them."

But mastering the NBA style didn't come easily. The greatest pros play an all-around game, where defense means almost as much as offense. Defense was something Hawkins had not studied as carefully as offense. He worked at it, though.

In the scoring column, Hawkins registered the totals expected of him. By the All-Star game, in which he played for the Western Division squad, the rookie sensation was averaging better than 23 points a game. He increased his scoring pace during the second half of the season, finishing his rookie year with a 24.6 points-per-game average. He earned the admiration of people who make sharp evaluations of the pros, people such as Red Holzman, coach of the New York Knickerbockers. "Hawkins is a complete player," Holzman said. "You have to like him, because he plays both ends of the floor. I'd hate to see him get any better—he's too good now."

Hawkins' driving play moved the Suns out of the cellar, where they had settled the season before. Yet, not everyone was in Connie's camp. A harsh appraisal was being made of his total play by some of the men he faced each game. San Diego's Elvin Hayes criticized Hawkins as a clown. "He's still got too much of the Globetrotter in him. In the NBA there are only two things to do with the ball—go to the hoop or pass it to a teammate."

Hawkins disagreed with that attitude. "If I get the ball in one hand and swing it, that makes the defensive player more concerned about what I might do than if I hold it in two hands, which minimizes my mobility. And if I see a man open, I want to get

*Big but agile, Connie dribbles around Bill Bradley of
the New York Knicks.*

the ball to him no matter where I'm holding it because he's only open for a split second."

As for his defensive game during the first half of
Hawkins' "break-in" season, a percentage of the
league's attitude was mirrored in the reactions of the

Knicks after they had defeated the Suns on a neutral court. Said Knick guard Dick Barnett, after scoring 23 points against Hawkins before Hawkins was shifted to defend against Bill Bradley, "I wish he had stayed on me longer. I would've gotten fifty."

Normally NBA players praised "the Hawk." Jerry West of the Los Angeles Lakers called Hawkins, "One of the three greatest players in the world." Kareem Abdul-Jabbar of the Milwaukee Bucks topped West by saying Connie is "the best I've ever played against anywhere." Em Bryant of the Boston Celtics offered perhaps the highest praise by saying that Hawkins is "better than Elgin Baylor."

Each man has a battle to win. Most have had it easier than Connie Hawkins, who had the cards stacked against him from the very beginning. But as each season passes and he continues to swoop in for buckets with the grace and power of a hawk in flight, cage fans will be reminded of his feelings about himself and the game he loves. "The big thing is, I got my chance now," Connie said as he got ready for his NBA debut. "I never went to jail. But I was sentenced to eight years in some kind of prison, waiting for a chance to prove myself. It was like dying of thirst with a faucet running in front of you and your hands tied behind your back. Now I've been cut free. I can reach out for what I want. I want to prove myself. Not to the NBA. Not to the press. Not to anyone but me. I got to prove me to me."

ELVIN
HAYES
by DAVE SENDLER

AS a schoolboy in Rayville, Louisiana, Elvin Hayes was shy, introverted and without friends. He was the kind of boy people say will never amount to anything. One day two older, stronger boys lured him from his house to beat him up and ridicule him for his speech impediment. The pain went deep.

Playing for the University of Houston in the Astrodome in January, 1968, Hayes seemed to be a different man. There the largest crowd in college basketball history—52,693 screaming fans—waited breathlessly for the showdown. UCLA with forty-seven straight victories was playing against Houston with seventeen victories in a row. And All-America Lew Alcindor (later known as Kareem Abdul-Jabbar) was pitting his skill against All-America Elvin Hayes.

Elvin swished long jumpers, and forged in for shots underneath the basket. He blocked a few shots back in Alcindor's face. With twenty-eight seconds left and the score 69-69, he sank two free throws. Houston won by that margin. In his duel with Alcindor Elvin's win was greater—39 points to 15, and 15 rebounds to 12.

Only Elvin Hayes appreciates how far he has come. His anguished progress from Rayville to Houston makes victory all the sweeter. But it also tempers his joy. He knows there'll be other ups—and other downs.

Since joining the San Diego Rockets of the National Basketball Association in the 1968-69 season, he has enjoyed mostly "ups." He led the league in scoring as a rookie. He made the All-Star team in each of his first two seasons. And his pay has been so lucrative that he purchased an $82,000, five-bedroom home.

But Elvin cannot wipe out the past. Perhaps that is what drives him to greatness on a basketball court.

His desire to succeed was obvious when he set out to prove himself in the NBA. He had college press clippings, and a six-figure contract, but he would need more than that to score baskets against Bill Russell or to outplay Wilt Chamberlain under the basket.

In his pro debut, Hayes went up against Seattle and tough Bob Rule. Elvin did not disappoint anyone. Although he didn't dominate the game, he scored 25 points as his San Diego team won. Rule

The victory over UCLA was more than a team triumph for Elvin. He made a name for himself nationally.

managed 31 points and helped to foul Hayes out of the ballgame. While Elvin respected Rule, he was unruffled. "I'm an inch taller," said Hayes. "I can relax against Rule. I can shoot my pet shots." When they met again, it was all Hayes. Elvin outscored, outrebounded, outplayed Rule.

Before facing Chamberlain for the first time, Hayes got a taste of San Francisco's Nate Thurmond and Baltimore's Leroy Ellis. Thurmond is an intimidator—stalking opponents, banging away their shots, using his muscle around the basket. Elvin chose to work around Nate with speed and agility rather than try to go chest-to-chest with him. When the game was over, Hayes had more than 30 points and Thurmond had less than 20. With his spring and movement, Elvin also pulled down more rebounds. Ellis was less of a challenge because he was too slight to bully Hayes and not fast enough to stay with him.

In his fifth professional game, Elvin came face-to-face with Chamberlain. A man of enormous size and strength, Chamberlain is at least four inches taller and 50 pounds heavier than Elvin. More than that, though, Chamberlain is a well-coordinated athlete who can move gracefully and shoot accurately. Hayes had had an opportunity to sample the Chamberlain treatment in an exhibition game. Though Wilt had taken it easy, Elvin had come away with some vivid memories. "Once Wilt went up for a dunk shot, his arm extended," recalled Elvin. "I never saw an arm like that. Unreal. I wondered, 'What am I doing here?' I got out of his way. One thing I know: I won't go up and agitate him."

In their first meeting in the regular season, the two crouched for the opening tip and up went the ball. Chamberlain tapped it to a teammate and the education of Elvin Hayes was underway. The Laker players came to the rookie, testing him. Freddie Crawford drove right in and banked in a layup. Then Wilt had the ball. He wheeled, drew a foul by Hayes, and tossed the ball in from short range. Soon after, Wilt picked off a rebound, leaped, and scored in one fluent motion. Again a Laker missed. Again Wilt went up to rebound the shot.

The Los Angeles players were whizzing toward the hoop like cars on a California freeway. Elgin Baylor zoomed in for a successful layup. From backcourt, Crawford slipped in to bang in a rebound. Wilt tipped in another shot.

Though thoroughly frustrated, Elvin Hayes would not quit. He had skills, confidence and—most important—staying power. Though jostled and harassed, he got off his shots, sometimes taking the jumper, sometimes daring to go right underneath the basket where Chamberlain was stationed. Elvin dropped in a 13-foot jump shot and another from near the foul line. Getting good position once, he tipped in a rebound.

When the game ended, the rookie had not pre-dominated. But neither had he crumbled. The final score was Lakers 152, San Diego 116. Chamberlain had poured in 28 points and cleared 23 rebounds to Hayes' 23 points and 9 retrieves.

"Intimidated?" Elvin said, echoing a reporter's post-game question about going against Wilt. "Inti-midated? You're not intimidated when you score twenty-three points."

Elvin was not just talking. In back-to-back games soon after that, he put in 40 points against the Chi-cago Bulls and 54 against the Detroit Pistons. Where he had been content to flip his jump shot and fall back, now he moved in, taking his shot, following the ball to the basket in case it was off target. The next time he went against Chamberlain, Hayes dropped in 38 points! Rather than be intimidated by Chamberlain, Hayes was actually helped.

Wilt talked to the rookie as they played. "He couldn't do enough to help me," said Hayes. "He didn't hold anything back either. He tells you the kind of shots you can make over him, the kind of shots he can block, and the kind you should be shooting depending on your ability. He never tells anything to hurt you. The amazing thing about the guy is he does all this as your opponent."

No one, really, stopped Hayes. He scored at a 28.4 points-a-game clip and led the league in point pro-duction during his rookie year. The last rookie to do that had been Chamberlain nine years earlier. On top of that, Elvin gathered in 17.1 rebounds per outing. The Rockets, who had won only fifteen games the previous season, won thirty-three in 1968-69 and made the playoffs.

Elvin continued with his All-Star play as a second-year man. He led all rebounders with a 16.9 per-game average and scored at a 27.5 clip, third-best in the NBA, but the Rockets fell back to last place. Elvin continued to play top ball the next two seasons —the first in San Diego and the second in Houston, where the Rockets moved in 1971. But the team missed the playoffs both years and it began to seem that Hayes might never play for a winner.

Then before the 1972-73 season Hayes was traded to the Baltimore Bullets. There he teamed up with Wes Unseld to give the Bullets top scoring and rebounding. After a slow start, the team finished fast, placing first in the Central Division. Hayes scored 21.2 points per game and averaged more than 14 rebounds.

Hayes' critics had always suggested he was too quick to get off a shot. "I don't take crazy shots," Elvin replied. The success of the Bullets may finally prove his value to a team, yet a few doubters persist.

Shaking off bad opinions was nothing new for Hayes. For there were lots of people in Rayville who thought young Elvin was just plain stupid. He didn't say much, to be sure, but people didn't realize

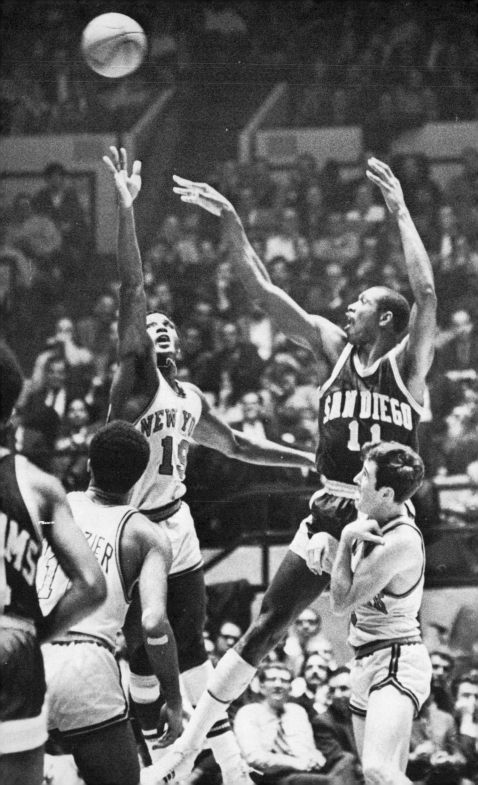

that Elvin's difficulty wasn't ignorance but a speech impediment.

Aware of how people felt about him, Elvin kept to himself. His closest relationship was with his father, who was a boiler supervisor in town. "Nobody wanted to associate with me," says Hayes. "Only my dad understood me. He really loved me." But Chris Hayes died when Elvin, the youngest of six children, was in ninth grade.

Meanwhile, Hayes had begun to play basketball. He had put up a tin can in back of his house and practiced throwing a rubber ball into it. By the time he was a high school freshman, he stood 6-feet 2-inches tall. He went out for the basketball team and was cut. He just couldn't seem to get out of his own way. The coach gently advised him to continue to work on his game.

Elvin took him at his word. The following summer, Hayes was on the court daily from 9 A.M. until 10 P.M. with a half-hour off for lunch. That was his routine six days a week. His mother forbade him to play on Sunday.

As a high school sophomore, Elvin once again tried out for the varsity. Once again he was cut. Undaunted he returned to the practice court to pre-

With high-scoring Elvin (No. 11) in the San Diego lineup, the Rockets more than doubled their number of victories in 1969.

pare for still another varsity tryout as a junior. By now, Hayes stood 6 feet 5 inches. This time, the coach kept him on the squad. By season's end, Elvin had scored 928 points and gathered in about 500 rebounds.

His growth continued in all respects. He sprouted another two inches before his last year in high school. After he scored 1,132 points, forty colleges expressed interest in enrolling him.

He chose the University of Houston, where he and Don Chaney became the first blacks to play for the basketball team. The decision took courage because many in Rayville wanted Elvin to go to one of the predominately Negro colleges in Louisiana and warned him that the whites would just be capitalizing on him at Houston. Elvin has admitted that one of the reasons he decided on Houston—which was relatively unknown at that time—was that if he failed, not too many people would know about it.

Still reserved and not accustomed to mingling with whites, Hayes went off to Houston. At first Houstonians thought of Elvin as a simple country boy because he stammered and had difficulty expressing what was on his mind. He met the communications problem head-on. He majored in speech and spent time at a Houston clinic helping kids who also had speech problems. He conquered his own difficulty and became a more outgoing, articulate man.

Hayes had no handicap on the basketball court. There was much to marvel at. Elvin shot with a soft touch and worked powerfully underneath. He broke the freshman scoring record. But he impressed people just as much with his defense. Gifted with great spring in his legs, Elvin would coil and wait for opponents to drive. When they made their moves, he would go high in the air and slap their shots aside.

In his first varsity year, Hayes averaged 27.2 points a game and began to attract national notice. The turning point for him that year came in a game against Dayton in Madison Square Garden. The opposing center was Henry Finkel, a 7-footer and a senior. Some experts felt that Hayes might be over-matched. When the game was over, they had different thoughts. Going over and around Finkel, Elvin got 20 points and 18 rebounds. Finkel scored just seven points and had only nine rebounds.

If Elvin had any doubts about how his white teammates felt about him, they were dispelled one night after a game against Centenary College in Shreveport, Louisiana. The Houston players had all gone into a restaurant and were just settling down when a waitress said some nasty things about Hayes and Chaney. Without hesitation, the whites on the team arose and filed out of the place.

The first encounter with Alcindor came in the NCAA semifinals when Elvin was a junior. Hayes surprised reporters with his pre-game comments.

The country boy was speaking out. He was saying that Alcindor, while a fine ballplayer, wasn't perfect. Elvin pointed out that Lew loafed on defense. "He has height, agility, and good coordination," said Hayes. "But I'm a pretty fair ballplayer myself. I can't say he's better than I am. As far as I am concerned, Lew Alcindor is just another guy."

In the game itself, UCLA was too much for Houston. The final score was 73-58. Elvin outscored Lew, 25-19, but he felt humiliated and wanted revenge.

That revenge came when the two met in that extravaganza in the Houston Astrodome. For Hayes, it was a satisfying team and personal victory. In all fairness though, it must be pointed out that Alcindor had played with an eye injury that is said to have blurred his vision.

The climax of that 1967-68 season came in Los Angeles when the two teams clashed in an NCAA semifinal game. Houston was undefeated and ranked number one in the country. UCLA was rated number two, having lost only to Houston. The Californians felt their loss had been a fluke and they were determined to prove it to Hayes and company.

It would be nice to say that Hayes rose to the challenge. But the fact was that Alcindor and UCLA would not be denied. In a forceful display of precision offense and tenacious defense, the Bruins ran Houston off the court, 101-69. Alcindor contributed 19 points, while Hayes scored a mere 10. Since Elvin

was the second most productive scorer in major-
college history (Oscar Robertson had been the only
player to top him in career points), it was a disap-
pointing finale. But Hayes had learned to accept the
downs as well as the ups.

Besides, the professional basketball teams were
waiting in the wings to cheer him up. Both of the
pro leagues wanted him badly and were willing to
pay huge sums of money to sign him. San Diego said
it would give him a contract worth $440,000. "I
never once thought of playing in the ABA, no matter
how much they'd offered," said Hayes later. He
agreed to terms with the Rockets.

Cheered by his good fortune at the bargaining
table, Elvin Hayes was still realistic enough to recog-
nize what he would have to contribute to make the
investment pay off. Just before his rookie season began, Elvin told a reporter, "Everybody is waiting for
me to fall on my face."

If there are people who wanted Elvin to fall on his
face in the pros, they have been sorely disappointed.

SPENCER HAYWOOD
by DAVE SENDLER

SPENCER HAYWOOD is a hard man to keep down.

As a teenage boy in Mississippi, he ran with a tough crowd and got little education at school. Yet he managed to get his high school diploma after he moved to Detroit.

He wanted to become the first black basketball player in the Southeastern Conference but never had a chance because his grades weren't good enough to get him into the University of Tennessee. Instead, he went to a junior college in Colorado, which was his springboard to the Olympic trials.

He played for a U.S. Olympic team that he and his teammates were told would be the first U.S. team to fail to win the gold medal. Spencer worked like a demon to help the U.S. win—and he became a national hero.

At the University of Detroit, he was on his way to becoming one of the most famous college basketball players ever, but personal and financial problems intervened. At age twenty, however, he signed a professional contract and now he may be set for life.

Spencer signed with the Denver Rockets of the American Basketball Association for $250,000—removing money as a problem for the Haywoods. Nevertheless, he decided to seek a college degree by arranging for classes in the off-season. Meanwhile, of course, there was the matter of establishing that he would be worth the quarter of a million dollars invested in him.

His professional debut came in 1969 against the Washington Caps, the defending ABA champs. Denver fans welcomed the 6-foot 9-inch rookie with a mighty roar. After a slow start, he began to give them something to cheer about. He grabbed rebounds with a special zeal, leaping high to nab the ball and trigger the Rockets' fast break. On offense, he moved with quickness and bounce, scoring well from inside. Down by 11 points in the third quarter, Denver crept back. The Rockets drew within five on a stuff shot by Haywood early in the fourth quarter and went on to win, 106-105. Haywood's 24 points were high for the Rockets.

In his second ABA game, Spencer provided further evidence that he would take hold right away. He led the team with 22 points, and, by clearing 26 rebounds, set a Denver record. There was plenty of room for refining some of his techniques, but he was clearly on his way to becoming Rookie of the Year. Who could deny a youngster who had paced his league in rebounding and scoring?

Beyond that, Spencer earned his money by drawing good crowds wherever he played in the ABA. Haywood became the most exciting drawing card in the league. He was doing a lot of good—for the league, for the team and for himself.

In his early teens though, Haywood did no one much good, least of all himself. Living with his mother and family in Silver City, Mississippi, he paid small attention to what was going on in school. The academic year amounted to six months; Spencer attended classes maybe half that time. He had trouble even writing his name as a teenager. With little to look forward to in life, he knocked around the country, moving between relatives in Chicago and Detroit. "I was headed the wrong way," Haywood recalled. "I was, you know, a thug. All I wanted to do was rob, or hustle a pool game, whatever it took to make some money."

He was fifteen and playing ball on a playground in Detroit one day when a fortuitous meeting turned his life around. Will Robinson, the basketball coach at Pershing High School in Detroit, spotted Spencer and began to ask him questions. Spencer told him he had a tenth-grade certificate from a school in Mississippi and that he had moved around a lot. Would he, inquired Robinson, consider settling down in Detroit?

Haywood said he would. With that, Robinson went to work. He contacted James and Ida Bell, a couple he knew with three children. The Bells agreed to take Spencer in and provide him with a legal residence. They gave him more. "He was so poor and backward," said Mrs. Bell. "Since his family couldn't help, we tried to love him as ours."

Robinson urged the teachers at Pershing High School to instruct Spencer on *how* to study as well as what to study. Haywood worked overtime with tutors to catch up on what he had missed in previous years. For pocket money, Spencer swept out the locker room and did odd jobs.

As a basketball player, Haywood had size (6 feet 6 inches), strength and speed. He could execute a variety of shots and moves on the court. He didn't, however, understand the rudiments of playing defense. Robinson recalled that when the other team had the ball, Spencer would just stand around flatfooted, his arms dangling without purpose.

Robinson taught him fundamentals. He insisted that Haywood practice ballet maneuvers to acquire grace of movement. The coach had Spencer running mile after mile to build up his endurance. "I started doing everything a coach does, a father does, a friend does," said Robinson. "Nobody had ever taken that kind of interest in Spencer before." For his part, Haywood called Will Robinson "the only father I've ever known."

The boy who had seemed to be going nowhere had direction now. Though just a high school boy, he played summertime basketball games against pros like Eddie Miles and Sonny Dove of the Detroit Pistons. At school, Spencer progressed both academically and athletically. His grades rose from a "D" average to nearly a "B" by graduation time. As a senior in 1967, Haywood led Pershing to the state championship and became a high school All-America.

The colleges came looking for him—400 of them. He decided on the University of Tennessee and said he wanted to become the first black basketball player in the Southeastern Conference. He signed a letter of intent and spent the summer being tutored in Knoxville. Will Robinson didn't approve of Spencer's choice. He didn't think Haywood was ready to handle the pressures of being a crusader. "I could advise him not to go to Tennessee," said Robinson, "but I couldn't make his decision for him." Spencer never matriculated at Tennessee—but not because he didn't want to. His summer preparation just wasn't productive enough and he failed the entrance examinations.

Haywood took the setback courageously. He enrolled at Trinidad Junior College in Colorado, where he studied as hard as he pursued his basketball. When the year was over, he had achieved a 3.2 average in the classroom—a solid "B." On the court, he scored 27.3 points a game, led all junior college players with 23.3 rebounds per outing, made Junior College All-America, and helped his team enjoy a 27-4 season.

Making a name for himself at Trinidad resulted in a chance to try out for the U. S. Olympic team in 1968. Spencer joined the first junior college group ever invited to the trials. He was the youngest of eighty-eight players bidding for spots on the twelve-member team.

Olympic play gets rough—a fouled player doesn't shoot his fouls for the first thirty-five minutes—and teams like the Armed Forces squad gave young Haywood a going-over. Four of them fouled out while bumping Spencer around. When the game was over, he had collected 24 points and 15 rebounds. The Armed Forces won, though, 86-80, and the junior college boys settled for fourth place in an eight-team tournament. Spencer had made mistakes, such as dribbling at the wrong time and shooting from too far out. But he was the best rebounder and third-highest scorer in the tournament. The Olympic officials found him more than adequate. He was selected for the trip to Mexico City.

The 1968 Olympic team was labeled as the worst

squad—in terms of talent—that the U. S. had ever fielded in the Games. No one really knew who Spencer Haywood was. What the fans did know was that All-America stars Lew Alcindor (Kareem Abdul-Jabbar), Elvin Hayes and Wes Unseld had elected not to try out for the team, and that other heralded stars like Rick Mount, Pete Maravich and Calvin Murphy had somehow been cut during the trials.

Spencer and the rest of the team worked tirelessly to blend their skills. They vowed they'd silence the critics, which they did. In fact, they swarmed all over the opposition in Mexico City. The U. S. won nine straight games and the gold medal. In the decisive game against Yugoslavia, the U. S. had gone off the floor at halftime with just a three-point lead. But then Haywood and teammate Jo-Jo White from Kansas took charge. Each scored eight points during a 17-point spree that pushed the American advantage to 20 points. Spencer finished with 23 points and the U.S. won, 65-50. When Spencer jogged off the floor just before the end of the game, the crowd rose and cheered him. Spencer was moved. "That's something that just not every player gets," he said proudly.

"Spencer has got to improve his passing and he's got to learn to take the turn in to the basket, but he's got everything else," said Olympic coach Hank Iba after the final game. "He could make it right now with most pro clubs."

Indeed, Spencer received offers to turn professional, but he had other ideas about how to plan his
life. He had decided to transfer to the University of
Detroit, announcing, "I'm going to get my diploma.
Even if it takes me five years, I'm going to get it. I
don't want people looking down on me as a guy who
is trying to cash in quick. I want to get an education."

He elected to major in radio and television, ready-
ing himself for a career as an actor or a disc jockey.
He collected three B's and a C in his first semester
and one of his school advisers, enthused by Haywood's performance in the classroom, called him
"unstoppable."

He was also unstoppable with his basketball uniform on. In his awesome debut for Detroit, he
soared high to ram in a stuff shot, which is illegal in
college, and wound up ripping down the glass backboard. "I was looking down through the basket and
I saw this guy waiting to submarine me," said Haywood. "So I grabbed the rim. It was an old backboard anyway."

The Detroit Titans won their first ten games.
Haywood seemed to do everything—scoring, running, passing, defending, rebounding. He swept up
and down the court with surpassing effect. He de-

*Spencer was pretty much an unknown until the
Olympics. Then he carried the U.S. team to victory
over Yugoslavia.*

stroyed the opposition in the Motor City Tournament, which the Titans hosted. Against Mississippi State, he accounted for 32 points and 29 rebounds during an 86-62 romp. He came back the next night with a machine gun burst that sent Temple University running for cover. Spencer pumped in the first ten shots he tried, and demoralized Temple never recovered. Detroit won both the game and the tournament.

The team climbed to seventh ranking in the nation and one of the boys on the team said, "With Spencer, we think we can do almost anything."

Then, however, reality intruded on the happy times of Spencer and his teammates. With his success, Haywood now attracted two and three defenders wherever he moved on offense. There was plenty of bumping and shoving. A superlative leaper, Haywood was getting frustrated by the rule forbidding dunk shots. To make matters worse, the team cooled off from its torrid start, losing seven of its next ten games.

The pressure was building up in the youngster, and Haywood boiled over twice in February. The first incident came after a loss to Notre Dame. Spencer caustically told a television interviewer, "I hate college basketball." Coach Bob Calihan, standing next to Spencer, was taken by surprise and did his best to divert the discussion to other subjects. Two days later, Spencer explained that he had been keenly disappointed when he made the remark. But he added that he wasn't sorry he had said what he did.

"If we had won Saturday, I wouldn't have said it," Spencer admitted. "I was never that upset about losing a game in my life. It's just losing. Our record here is bad. I've lost more games this year than I've lost all my life."

"I think it was just the frustration of losing a tough game," said Calihan. "He's had to adjust to the defenses."

The second blowup got national attention. Just before a game with the University of Toledo, Spencer had announced his intention of trying to break the Detroit record of 44 points in a game. He made the game memorable, all right, but not because of his scoring.

Early in the second half, he and Toledo's Steve Mix made vigorous contact after going up for a rebound. The two fell out of bounds and shoved at each other. Referee George Strauthers described what followed: "Haywood and Mix were struggling on the floor under the basket, and I called a jump ball. There was some scuffling, and a Toledo player, Larry Smith, and a Detroit player, Larry Moore, were coming in to help break up the two. But Haywood suddenly charged and began to swing at Smith. It was a flagrant foul, and I called, 'You're out of the game,' to Haywood. I called a second technical when he started swinging at me. I blocked him three times. He was swinging those haymakers. Guess he was lucky he didn't know where they were going. I talked to him later and he was very sorry for his actions."

Spencer later apologized to the referee, the Toledo team, and its coach. "I lost my control," said Spencer about his attack on the referee. "I got angry about what I felt was an unfair accusation that I struck another player. I made a mistake. I am very sorry for what I did."

Haywood drew a week's suspension for his misconduct. He missed games against Xavier and Baldwin-Wallace. Then he came back to finish up the season. His final statistics told one facet of his sophomore year. They demonstrated that there were few players who could match his skill, for Spencer had led the nation with 21.5 rebounds a game and had ended up fourth in scoring with a 31.8 average. Naturally, he was an All-America.

There was, however, another story to be played out. That one involved his probable disillusionment with what he had expected college ball to be. His concern for the welfare of his mother and his brothers and sisters was a factor, too. At any rate, in

Haywood is not big as centers go. But his springy legs enable him to block shots or do any of the chores of a near 7-footer.

August, Spencer stunned the sports world by announcing that he was quitting the University of Detroit to play for the Denver Rockets of the ABA. Haywood was reported to have signed for $250,000. He said he did it so his mother "won't have to be scrubbing floors for $10 a week." Spencer said he had promised Will Robinson he would attend college classes in the off-season and get his degree within three years.

The ABA justified drafting Spencer out of school by citing a league rule permitting a player to be signed before his class graduates in case of extreme hardship. The University of Detroit reacted with anger.

The deed, however, was done. Soon the furor died down and people were just talking about Spencer's basketball. Sam Balter, a member of the 1936 Olympic basketball team and more recently a play-by-play announcer for the ABA's Los Angeles Stars, said, "Spencer Haywood is on his way to developing into the perfect player. He's a composite of all those people we call superstars." Balter, who was particularly impressed with Haywood's aggressive defense, added, "I've actually seen him leap and intercept a field goal try more than twenty feet away from the basket. Nobody else has ever done that. Haywood is the best jumper in the history of the game."

But by the end of his first season with Denver, Spencer was unhappy. He felt that his contract promised more than it delivered and that he was worth more elsewhere.

Before the 1970-71 season began, Haywood announced that he was jumping from Denver to the Seattle Supersonics in the NBA. He became the center of a legal storm as the two leagues *and* the individual teams in the NBA fought over him.

Haywood's contract with Seattle was finally approved, but by the time the legal knots were untied he had missed half the season. He came back in 1971-72 to average 26 points per game. And Seattle had its first winning season ever although it missed the playoffs. The fans were looking forward to an even better season in 1972-73.

The new season was a big disappointment. Player-coach Lenny Wilkens was traded away from Seattle and the team was torn by dissension. Only Spencer had a good year. He averaged 29.2 points per game and led the team in rebounds. But the Sonics finished with a 26-56 won-lost record.

At the end of his fourth pro season, Spencer was about to celebrate his 24th birthday. It was hard to remember that the "veteran" had come so far at such a young age. He had not yet won any team a championship—but with his spectacular talent it seemed only a matter of time.

LOU
HUDSON
by LOU SABIN

THE basketball court was outdoors. The playing surface wasn't wood; instead, it was bumpy ground with patches of grass. A makeshift hoop was nailed to a tree, and it rattled as the ball banged against the rim before dropping through. With each goal the cheer that followed wasn't from the throats of thousands of people, but from a handful of delighted, appreciative fans who had taken time out from a war to watch some professionals play their game.

The year was 1969. The place was Vietnam. The player who had just made the two-pointer was Lou Hudson of the Atlanta Hawks. Along with such NBA stars as Wes Unseld of the Baltimore Bullets, Jon McGlocklin of the Milwaukee Bucks and Elvin Hayes of the San Diego Rockets, Hudson, by his own admission, was "bringing a bit of home to guys over there." He said the trip was one of the most fantastic experiences he had ever had.

There were many moments in the life and career of Lou Hudson which he could have chosen as "most fantastic." But the mark of this man is his concern about others as well as himself. To have brought some moments of relaxation to war-weary soldiers was a good thing for him to do, a selfless thing to do. It was as typical of his personality as his reluctance to take more than his "share" of shots in any game.

"Louis was always a quiet, unselfish person," said a man who has known and admired Hudson since his boyhood days in Greensboro, North Carolina. "Most of the athletes let fame go to their heads. Not Louis. He's a good man who has always taken care of his folks and kept in touch with his high school coach."

Hudson's coach at Dudley High School, Bill Furcron, will never forget the sight of young Lou, as the rebounding and scoring leader on teams that won numerous titles, including the state's Negro high school championship. Lou gave his coach, his school, his parents and the city of 150,000 a lot to be proud of. He also gave Irwin Smallwood, then the Executive Sports Editor of the Greensboro *Daily News,* something special to write about. After watching Lou in action for the first time, Smallwood said, "Louis would get the rebound, bring it down court, shoot, score, and go back for another rebound. He scored twenty points in the first sixteen minutes

I saw him play. He reminded me of Tom Gola, Doug Moe—those guys who were the first of the smoothies."

The schoolboy star was smooth all right. But more than that, he was amazingly accurate at putting the ball through the net. Even when he was young Hudson was confident on the court. "In high school," he said, "I used to feel that nobody could shoot better than I. And this kept my interest in basketball. Until the ninth grade, I switched sports with the seasons. I played football, baseball and basketball. I stopped baseball then and played basketball from the end of one football season to the beginning of the next. For some reason, I originally wanted to play football the most. Although it's been written that I was a great high school quarterback, the truth is, I was not. It was Mr. Furcron who convinced me my best future was in basketball."

Furcron contributed to Lou's development in several ways. He developed a drill that Hudson never stops practicing. "Mr. Furcron would pair me against a guard every chance he got," says Lou, who was then a forward. "This pairing resulted in the development of quickness which equalizes things when I'm matched against someone bigger than I am."

Now one of the biggest NBA guards—a bruiser in the backcourt at 6 feet 5 inches and 220 pounds—Lou is exceptionally agile.

The publicity that came after Smallwood's "discovery" of Hudson started Lou on the path that would eventually lead to fame, the NBA, and a sizeable salary. But such a future would have been hard to predict when Lou was born in Greensboro, July 11, 1944. Both of his parents worked—his father in a pajama factory, his mother as a domestic—to support Lou, another son and five daughters. When Lou wasn't studying, taking part in school affairs, or polishing his talents on basketball courts, he was earning money by shining shoes at a downtown newsstand.

Then came Dudley High basketball, and the shooting star's comet began to soar. College scholarship offers began filling the mailbox, inviting Lou to campuses everywhere in the nation. He selected the University of Minnesota.

Lou quickly showed Coach John Kundla he wasn't just another schoolboy hotshot who collapsed under the pressure of college competition. While making his Big Ten debut against Purdue as a sophomore, Hudson cracked his head open in a collision with the backboard. As he crumpled to the floor, a heavy silence blanketed the stands. But Lou simply got up, had the injury patched, and came roaring back to notch 15 of the Minnesota Gophers' next 20 points. With this kind of courage and shooting spearheading their drive, the Gophers fought from behind to win the game.

Hudson played hard to win, but he preferred

getting the ball by clever means rather than by rough-housing under the boards. Basketball, he felt, is a sport of finesse and skill. "I'd rather take a man one-on-one and beat him, or watch a teammate do it," he said. "That's one of the things that make this a really fine game."

Hudson was Minnesota's top scorer as a sophomore. However, he also learned that it takes overall development before a sharpshooter can consider himself a complete player. After another season as the Gophers' prime point-maker, Lou played for the United States team in the Student Olympics Tournament in Budapest, Hungary, along with Princeton's Bill Bradley. "I think I've really learned to be more of a total player," Lou said. "You pick up little things, like running a man off a pick instead of trying to beat him on sheer speed. If a coach tells you to do something, it may sound right or it may not—but it never makes the same impression as when you see someone your own age do it. And I also found out in Budapest that five individuals can learn to play together, even without much practice, and that it doesn't make much difference how you do individually as long as your team wins."

Hudson's unselfish play from that day on underscores how well he learned the rules of team play. In his senior year, Hudson was dramatically forced to put on a display of spirit and ability that will forever be a part of Minnesota basketball history. During

the fifth game of the schedule, he broke his shooting arm. When his arm was put in a cast, he was told he couldn't play for at least sixty days. Most players would accept the verdict, but Hudson didn't. "I kept going to practice," he recalled, "and begging the coach to let me play. Finally I convinced him I could handle the ball with the cast on."

Wearing a slightly lighter cast, Hudson rejoined the team for a game against Indiana. By the final buzzer the dedicated youngster, who should have been a spectator in street clothes, had connected on 50 per cent of his shots and scored a total of 20 points. He did it by using his cast-enclosed right hand to support his left hand for catching passes, dribbling and throwing up the ball.

When the NBA started grading the country's best collegians for its 1966 draft, Lou got high marks. During his junior year he had set a Minnesota single-season scoring record of 588 points, for a 23.3 points-per-game average. Additional honors included All-Big Ten three times, and All-America honors once. Lou would have shattered the Gophers' all-time scoring record if his arm hadn't been broken. As it was, he ended up just six points short of that total.

Richie Guerin, coach of the Hawks, had been

Lou, moving the ball against Ohio State All-America Gary Bradds, set all sorts of records at Minnesota.

measuring Lou's potential as a pro, and his decision was clear at the draft meeting. Picking fourth in the first round, Guerin tabbed Hudson as the man the Hawks, then based in St. Louis, wanted most.

Lou moved into the pro ranks with the same point-making flair he had displayed in earlier debuts. Playing eighty games at forward, he racked up an average of 18.4 points a game. He led all Hawk scorers. He also finished in second place in post-season voting for Rookie of the Year.

Before the next season began, the U.S. Army requested Lou's services for duty in the reserves. He spent five months going through military drills, wearing heavy boots instead of sneakers, and trying to stay in shape for basketball. When he did rejoin the Hawks, half the season was gone and the edge was off his game. Hudson appeared in forty-six contests that 1967-68 season and his scoring average dropped to 12.5 points per game. He did regain his touch in the playoffs, though, averaging 21.7 points for six games.

Nothing interfered with his progress the next season. He blistered the baskets at a rate of 21.9 points a game, recapturing his title as king of the Hawk scorers, and maintained a 22.0 point pace in each of eleven playoff games. His statistics were even more impressive because the team—now the Atlanta Hawks—was defense-oriented. Lou's 49.2 shooting percentage and 1,770 points earned him fifteenth place in the 1968-69 league scoring race. And his game-after-game consistency also won him a spot on the West squad in the All-Star game. Still, one teammate pointed out, "Lou doesn't shoot as much as we'd like him to. He connects on nearly half his shots, so he should take more. He seems kinda shy, like he doesn't want someone to say he's a gunner."

When confronted with his teammate's remarks about being afraid he might be called a "gunner," Hudson answered, "If you're a scorer like me, you need to make a high percentage of your shots. If you don't, your teammates might wonder if they shouldn't be shooting themselves, instead of passing to you."

However, Coach Guerin had plans for his All-Star forward in 1969-70, which meant that Hudson would handle the ball more than ever. In the playoffs the previous season, Guerin had shifted Lou from frontcourt to backcourt. During the first game Hudson played at guard, he met Jerry West of the Los Angeles Lakers face-to-face. West, almost impossible to handle under normal circumstances, was sheer murder in playoff matches. Only this time he made a skimpy 34 per cent of his shots and was held to 75 points over four games by Hudson. At the same time, Lou was totaling 92 points and sinking nearly 50 per cent of his shots. Guerin made clear his intentions for the future. "That did it for me," Guerin said. "From then on, he was a guard."

Starting Hudson in the backcourt for the 1969-70 season, Guerin looked like a genius. By mid-season, Lou was scoring at a 25.5 points-per-game clip, Atlanta was leading the Western Division, and the raves for Hudson were louder than ever. And by season's end, Hudson's 25.4 per-game clip had earned him fifth place in the league scoring race and a first-team rating on the All-Star five.

In an early November contest against the tall, tough Chicago Bulls, Lou took 34 shots—far more than his usual number. He sank 25 of them—close to 75 per cent success—and added seven free throws for a grand total of 57 points. Not only had he tied the long-standing Hawk single-game scoring record set by the incomparable Bob Pettit, he also received credit for eight assists. Atlanta won the game by one point.

"How do you stop a guy like that?" Dick Motta, the Chicago coach, moaned. Motta *had* tried everything to cool Hudson's hot hand, using four different players, including defensive whiz Jerry Sloan to cover Lou. But nothing worked. Lou figured in the winning goal without touching the ball. Chicago's Chet Walker had made two foul shots with nine seconds left on the clock, giving the Bulls a one-point edge. Atlanta called time out in order to set up one last play for Hudson. The Bulls, of course,

Lou leaps over the Boston Celtics' Tom Sanders, who seems surprised to see Hudson so high in the air.

were not fooled. They practically sent their whole team out to envelop Lou. But Walt Hazzard of the Hawks spotted Bill Bridges unguarded underneath the basket, passed the ball to him, and Bridges sank the game-winning shot.

That scoring splurge was a signal for the praise sung about Hudson to reach greater intensity. From the Baltimore Bullets' assistant coach, Bob Ferry, came these words: "Lou Hudson is basketball's greatest offensive machine." Walt Hazzard, Hudson's backcourt partner, said, "Lou, in time, is going to be the best ballplayer in this league. Right now, Lou's better than Jerry West of the Los Angeles Lakers, although Jerry's got a few years more behind him and has been injured a lot."

Hudson and West had a chance to compare talents when they played alongside each other for the first time in the 1969-70 All-Star game. Which man came out better is described by the box score: In thirty-one minutes of play, Jerry West made 22 points; in just eighteen minutes, Hudson hit for 15. Immediately after the game, a player who guarded both West and Hudson, said, "Sweet Lou's superior to Jerry. You really have to hound Lou, crowd him all the time. If you don't, he'll shoot you dead. He can hit on just about any shot twenty feet or less from the basket—and he's almost as deadly from more than twenty, too!"

Hudson's move to a guard position didn't automatically guarantee that he would shoot more and score more. At one point in the 1969-70 season, Hudson took a mere 37 shots in three games—and the Hawks lost all three. Lou's teammates insisted he shoot more. "Coach Guerin ordered me to move around more, to get involved in what was going on when we were on offense," recalled Hudson. "But Bill Bridges and Walt Hazzard were more specific. They told me I had better start shooting more. So when we played Cincinnati, after five straight losses, I made up my mind to work myself into position and then shoot every time I had the shot."

The result was that Hudson hit on 14 of 28 from the floor, outscored the great Oscar Robertson, 33-19, and snapped Atlanta out of the losing streak with a 117-110 victory.

Hudson soon learned that his success as a scorer paralleled the Hawks' success in the win-loss column. At one point in 1970, he put together three great scoring nights in a row, all of which Atlanta won. In his next game, it seemed as if Lou would cool off because of an injury to his shooting hand. He played a miserable first half with the bandaged hand. During the intermission, though, he discarded the bandage and went on to score 20 more points in the game and Atlanta won again. In the four-game stretch, he had accumulated 157 points. No one dared suggest that he was a "gunner." Instead, he was the same old team player he had always been.

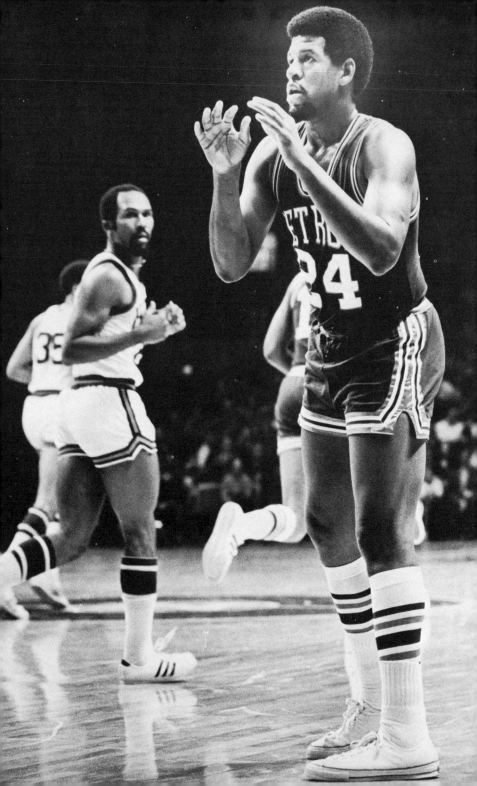

JIMMY WALKER

by DAVE SENDLER

THE professional basketball scouts who saw Jimmy Walker cavort for Providence College could see no way in which Walker could fail as a pro. In fact, when Walker completed his college career in 1967, the Detroit Pistons not only made him the very first draft choice, they gave him an astounding $250,000 contract in eager anticipation of the value they would receive.

Just watching Jimmy in New York's Holiday Festival in 1967 had indicated to the Pistons what they were getting. For here was a clutch player taking command. With Providence losing, 55-48, in the finals against St. Joseph's of Philadelphia, the 6-foot 3-inch, 205-pound guard turned it on. Using a fast, hard dribble, he jockeyed for position and let the ball fly. Swish! In quick succession, he snapped off two more jumpers. Again they dropped in. Within

127

eleven minutes, Jimmy pumped in 14 points and fed his teammates for four more baskets.

With 1:30 left on the scoreboard, St. Joe's was still in the game, trailing only 75-73. Up the court came Walker, unruffled as he wheeled with the ball through the opponent's pressing defense.

He signaled to his teammates across the midcourt line to clear the right side for him so he could go one-on-one with his man. Then his pace quickened. He feinted and drove hard for the basket. He got by his man, but two St. Joe's players leaped to stop him. As they did, Jimmy snaked a pass through to Mike Riordan who was all alone under the basket. Riordan's shot went through and he was fouled. When he converted the free throw, the score was 78-73 and Providence's lead was safe. The Friars won, 82-76. For the second straight year, Walker was the Festival's Most Valuable Player.

Jimmy had averaged 30.4 points a game during the 1966-67 college season, leading the nation. He drew such raves as:

". . . Great, fantastic, unbelievable . . . He can't miss being an outstanding pro."—Bob Cousy, then the coach of Boston College.

"He's a terrific shooter, fine passer and is as close to being the perfect player as I have ever seen."—

Walker collects the coveted MVP trophy at the Holiday Festival in New York after leading Providence to victory.

John Orr, then coach of the University of Massa-
chusetts.

. . . And so on.

So Jimmy Walker, All-America, first draft choice,
brought his act into the National Basketball Association in 1967-68. And to the disbelief of experts
around the nation, he failed miserably. He eked out
only 8.8 points a game and watched much more basketball from the bench than he did from midcourt.
Some of his followers, along with wishful thinkers in
the Pistons' front office, hoped it was just a rookie's
confusion. "Watch out for his second year, now that
he has learned his lessons," they said. But cold statistics show that Jimmy Walker didn't exactly merit
his fancy salary in 1968-69, either. His scoring average was a poor 11.7, and his play was leaden. This
wasn't the agile boy who had dribbled, passed, and
shot defenses out of business in college. There had
to be an explanation. There was.

Jimmy had joined up with a team that already had
a playmaker to quarterback the attack. Dave Bing,
also young and exceptionally quick, had established
himself as one of the league's brightest stars. Dave
could shoot outside, penetrate, and make all the
plays. Jimmy had to fall into orbit around Bing, al-
lowing the veteran to have the ball most of the time
and control the tempo of the game. So Jimmy re-
treated into the background.

Jimmy also had trouble getting along with coach

Donnis Butcher and Butcher's successor, Paul Seymour. "I wouldn't call them run-ins," he said of his
problems with his coaches. "It was more personality
differences."

In all fairness to Butcher and Seymour, they were
frustrated to watch a player with Walker's talent
flounder on the court. Jimmy had gotten down on
himself and, not playing full-time, had allowed his
weight to balloon to 225. He wasn't as quick—nor,
it seems, as responsible as the Pistons wanted him to
be. He missed a plane and a game in the 1968-69
season and his delinquencies cost him money in
fines.

"During Jimmy's two years of troubles," said Detroit general manager Ed Coil, "a lot of people came
to us. They wanted to take him off our hands. But
they didn't want to give us anything of value."

Detroit brought in Butch van Breda Kolff as
coach for 1969-70. The new coach cleared the air for
Walker when he said publicly, "I had heard all the
stories about Jimmy. But he knows how to play this
game. I don't know what might have bothered him
and I'm not knocking anybody. But as far as I'm
concerned, we're starting from scratch."

For an actual start, Jimmy and Butch made a bet
with each other. The 211-pound van Breda Kolff
and Walker both had to come to training camp at
205. Each made it, and Jimmy announced in camp,
"My mental attitude has improved. I didn't think it

needed to be improved, but it has. I guess the weight loss has a lot to do with it."

Then Jimmy went out and played basketball the way he used to. Bing was out of the lineup at the time because of a knee injury. In addition, Bing had stated that he would eventually jump to the Washington team in the American Basketball Association. Thus, the Piston players looked to Jimmy as the leader of the future. He didn't disappoint them. Though Detroit continued to lose games and Bing did return to action, Walker kept right on playing the kind of basketball that eventually led him into the All-Star game.

In Saginaw, Michigan, on September 29, 1969 the "real" Jimmy Walker made his debut. The Pistons were playing the New York Knickerbockers in a pre-season game. There was Jimmy Walker weaving in and out of traffic, moving the ball, and getting the flow of the Detroit offense in motion. He was pounding in on the fast break, laying the ball up and in. Now he was slowing the pace down, then whipping the ball underneath for a teammate's easy basket. Up he'd go for that outside jumper. And the ball was going in—the way it did at Providence. Jimmy Walker was back. He tossed in 11 of 17 shots from the floor, made all 11 of his free throws, and got 7 assists as well. He felt like flying into the dressing room after the game. He didn't have to. Instead, jubilant teammate McCoy McLemore carried him there—a tribute to Jimmy's outstanding performance in the 124-122 victory.

Walker's reversal of form was no one-game fluke. Jimmy stayed at top form. By mid-season, he was named to play in the NBA All-Star game. He went on to average 21 points a game for the season. He had finally become the scorer and floor man that everybody knew he could be.

During one swing through the West in early December, Jimmy showed the league what a turned-on Walker could do. The first stop was Phoenix and Jimmy came out firing. He would dribble one way, then another. With his man scrambling to keep up, Walker would pull up and arch his quick jump shot for the hoop. Or he would penetrate inside, go up, and bank the ball off the board. Walker was making offense everywhere. He finished with 30 points and the game was Detroit's, 118-113.

Detroit moved on to San Diego the next night and Jimmy's shootout with Elvin Hayes & Company riddled the Rockets. Popping baskets from all over, Walker threw in 32 points and again Detroit won, 110-102. That was the most Jimmy had ever scored as a pro.

Still on the move, the Pistons hurried off to Seattle for their third game in three nights. They were a weary band, but fortunately they had their hot shooting hand along. Walker kept Detroit in the game with his passing and shooting. Although the

Pistons faded and lost, 109-104, Jimmy poured in 33 points. He had a new personal high.

The schedule permitted the Pistons a day off to fly home. Then Cincinnati came in to play and Jimmy greeted the Royals with a 30-point burst. He carried the club to a 119-116 victory.

By the All-Star break in January—after forty-eight games—Jimmy Walker was Detroit's leading scorer with a 21.1 average. He had made remarkable plays and improved upon his defense from the two previous years. Explaining his improvement, Walker said, "When I play more, my teammates begin to have confidence in me. It also helps to keep my weight down. I wasn't able to react to situations properly last year."

Getting into the NBA groove had been a struggle. But Jimmy Walker was used to struggles—he had been fighting all his life for a chance to prove himself. Jimmy had grown up in the Roxbury section of Boston, a Negro ghetto where chances of success are slim. A friend whom Jimmy had known since he was five, for example, is now in jail. He held up a store and killed a clerk. "I know a lot of guys with records," said Walker. "I was just lucky. It could have been me. They just weren't as fortunate as I've been."

Walker's chance to escape the bad influences of Roxbury came when he was 14. Jimmy was playing basketball on the playground when an older guy

joined the group. The stranger happened to be Sam
Jones of the Boston Celtics. The pro star got into
the pick-up game that was going on. "I was just out
for some exercise," Jones recalled, "and this skinny
kid gave me all I could handle." The skinny kid was
Jimmy Walker.

Sam took a personal interest in Jimmy. A warm
relationship developed. Sam lived only a block from
the playground and Jimmy lived six streets away. "It
got so," Walker said, "that I would drop in on his
house, not because he was a professional basketball
player, but it was the way he treated me. He was
friendly."

The times weren't easy for Walker. One night, for
example, he and five friends were going to a party.
"We're walking along," Jimmy remembers, "and
the cops picked us up. Somebody else had snatched a
pocketbook, but here's a bunch of kids doing nothing and they take us in. We were released in about
an hour and a half. But we were still picked up because it's that kind of thing, and we were Negro.
Now I look back and think how lucky I was . . ."

Jimmy was going to a trade school at the time,
living only for his basketball and his friendship with
Sam Jones. Jimmy's basketball coach at school was
probably well-meaning, but he said something to
Jimmy that hurt very much. The man told Jimmy
not to dream about going off to college, but to con-
centrate on learning a trade. "I was in the cabinet-

making department in the school and I wasn't doing well," Walker has admitted. "I just wasn't interested in cabinet-making. I knew I could do high school work. It was a mistake for me to go to a trade school. Right then I knew I had to get out of there. One year was enough, too much."

Sam Jones recognized the problem and took action. He suggested to Jimmy that he go to Sam's old high school, Laurinburg Institute, in North Carolina. Walker said it was out of the question because his parents couldn't afford to send him to a prep school.

"The next thing I knew," Jimmy says, "Sam was giving me the money." Walker got a partial scholarship to the school, but Sam Jones paid his tuition at $500 a year. More than that, Sam saw to it that Jimmy had a little spending money at school. "If he didn't send me money, his wife did," Jimmy recalls. "I'd go to the mailbox and there would be $15 from him for no reason."

Walker was able to do the classroom work at the school. He blossomed as a basketball player, too. In his two years at Laurinburg, Walker's team won forty-nine out of fifty games.

He didn't exactly get high-pressure recruiting from Providence, though. In fact, one would have to say he tagged along as an afterthought. Coach Joe Mullaney had a prospect named Bill Blair. Bill just happened to be Walker's cousin. One day, when Mullaney was at Blair's house, Mrs. Blair said, "What about cousin Jamie?" Mullaney looked into the matter of cousin Jamie—and got more than he could ever have hoped for.

At a school that had produced such outstanding professional guards as Lenny Wilkens and Johnny Egan, Walker stepped right in and gave every indication that he would generate backcourt excitement in the Providence tradition. He scored 22 points a game for the freshman team and varsity coach Mullaney glowed. Mullaney said he was especially pleased at the cool and steady way Jimmy played under pressure.

As a sophomore, Walker took charge of the Providence attack. Mullaney wanted Jimmy to bring the ball upcourt and deal it off to an open man when he couldn't get a shot himself. "In a situation such as this," Mullaney said, "his unselfishness was his biggest asset." One night, Mullaney remembers, he wanted Walker as a decoy. Jimmy faithfully followed orders. He took only three shots all night and scored just four points. But, points out Mullaney, Walker was just happy that the team won. He wound up his first varsity year averaging 20.5 points a game.

In his junior year, he was more spectacular. The most dramatic moment came in the finals of the Holiday Festival in New York's Madison Square Garden. Providence was matched against Boston Col-

lege, coached by Bob Cousy. "Jimmy's game," said Mullaney, "is one-on-one. He practices it with our big men, our small men, our fast men." Boston College stacked its defense on Walker, but found out he was capable of going one-on-*five*. He shot from outside, flipped jumpers from the sides, and pierced the defense for drives up the middle. When his *tour de force* was over, he had 50 points and Boston College was defeated, 91-86. Said Cousy, "What can you say about him? We knew how good he was before the game and we built our defense around him. We realized he'd get his thirty points, maybe even forty if he came up with a hot hand. But fifty—whoever thought of it?"

The 50-point output tied Oscar Robertson's Holiday Festival scoring record for a single game. Cousy was quick to admit that Jimmy was "the nearest thing to Oscar Robertson I've ever seen in college." For the season, he scored 24.5 points a game and made All-America.

As a senior, Walker continued his pattern of improvement—and he moved into a class by himself. He returned to Madison Square Garden for the Holiday Festival and in the very first game, he took Duquesne apart with his blazing shooting. He scored 37 points. Duquesne player Moe Barr, who chased

Walker, dribbling against Duquense, was a superb floor leader for Providence and later for the Pistons.

Jimmy all over the court, said later, "I tried everything to defense him. I even held his pants. Not even that worked." When Walker came off the floor just before the end of the Friars' 82-55 victory, the crowd of 14,636 stood and roared its approval of him. The ovation lasted for one full minute.

There was no let-up all season for Walker. By ringing up 73 points in his last two games, he beat out Lew Alcindor of UCLA for the national scoring title.

The Detroit Pistons eagerly signed him as the NBA's first draft choice. When the Pistons contracted to pay him a quarter of a million dollars someone asked Walker, "Do you feel rich now? Affluent?"

"No, just satisfied," he replied. "That was financial pleasure." It wasn't until he struggled into his third pro season that Jimmy Walker felt satisfied with himself as an athlete. Surprisingly, it had taken a while. But Jimmy Walker is now making up for lost time.

INDEX

....

Page numbers in italics refer to photographs

141